Praise for HUNDREDS OF HEADS™ *Survival Guides*

"A concept that will be . . . a huge seller and a great help to people. I firmly believe that today's readers want sound bytes of information, not tomes. Your series will most definitely be the next 'Chicken Soup.'"

—CYNTHIA BRIAN
TV/RADIO PERSONALITY, BEST SELLING AUTHOR: CHICKEN SOUP FOR THE GARDENER'S SOUL; BE THE STAR YOU ARE!; THE BUSINESS OF SHOW BUSINESS

"Move over, 'Dummies' . . . Can that 'Chicken Soup!' Hundreds of Heads are on the march to your local bookstore!"

—ELIZABETH HOPKINS
KFNX (PHOENIX) RADIO HOST, THINKING OUTSIDE THE BOX

Advance Praise for

HOW TO SURVIVE YOUR TEENAGER

"With warmth, humor and 'I've been there' compassion, editors Gluck and Rosenfeld have turned the ordinary experiences and struggles of parents into bits of compact wisdom that are easy to pick up and use straightaway. I especially liked this book's many examples of how to survive (and even thrive) while living under the same roof as your teen."

—JACLYNN MORRIS, M.ED.
CO-AUTHOR OF I'M RIGHT. YOU'RE WRONG. NOW WHAT?
AND FROM ME TO YOU

"The book really gave me some insight on my life and hopefully my parents will read it so we can enhance our relationship."

—DAVID E. WEINSTEIN
10TH GRADE CLASS PRESIDENT, RIVERWOOD HIGH SCHOOL
SANDY SPRINGS, GEORGIA

T0160630

Praise for other titles in the HUNDREDS OF HEADS *Survival Guide series*

HOW TO SURVIVE YOUR FRESHMAN YEAR

"This book proves that all of us are smarter than one of us."
> —JOHN KATZMAN
> FOUNDER AND CEO, PRINCETON REVIEW

"This book is right on the money. I wish I had this before I started college."
> —KATIE LEVITT
> SENIOR, GEORGE WASHINGTON UNIVERSITY

"Refreshingly funny and smart. After finishing *How to Survive Your Freshman Year*, I feel like I'm ready to take on the world. OK, maybe not, but almost. Like always having Pepto-Bismol in your medicine cabinet, you should have *How to Survive Your Freshman Year* ready whenever you run into a crisis."
> —VOX: THE VOICE OF OUR GENERATION (MAY 2004)

"Good advice about saying goodbye to your parents, dealing with homesickness, making new friends, and getting around campus. Should you live in a dorm or off campus? What activities will fit you? What about a roommate? Yikes! If you were a good student in high school, should you take extra classes or wait until you get your bearings? Oh, yeah, and what about studying? Alone or with groups? Is it really necessary to attend every class? These questions and lots more (money, laundry, food, sex, parties, time-management, etc.) are addressed with honesty and humor. This would be a great book to have for the graduating high school seniors to make them less anxious about college."
> –NORMA LILLY
> M.L.S., INGRAM LIBRARY SERVICE, "HIDDEN GEM" (JULY 2004)

"I was nervous about starting college, but now that I've read this book I feel totally confident."
> —JON BIRNBREY, SENIOR
> RIDGEWOOD HIGH SCHOOL
> ATLANTA, GEORGIA

HOW TO SURVIVE DATING

"'Be yourself' may be good dating advice, but finding Mr. or Ms. Right usually takes more than that. For those seeking more than the typical trite suggestions, the new book *How to Survive Dating* has dating tips from average folks across the country. It's like having a few hundred friends on speed-dial."
—KNIGHT RIDDER/TRIBUNE NEWS SERVICE (KRT)

"Great, varied advice, in capsule form, from the people who should know—those who've dated and lived to tell the tale."
—CARY TENNIS
COLUMNIST, SALON.COM

"A wonderful book, with thought-provoking advice—I'm going to recommend it to all my members. It gives valuable perspectives from others in the dating world. A one-stop shop for dating tips!"
—SARAH KATHRYN SMITH
OWNER, EIGHT AT EIGHT DINNER CLUB—A BETTER WAY TO MEET!

"Reading *How to Survive Dating* is like having a big circle of friends in one room offering their hard-earned advice about the toughest dating dilemmas. From the first kiss to knowing when it's time to say 'I love you,' this book can help you avoid the headaches and heartaches of dating. *How to Survive Dating* is a must-read for singles."
—THE WAUKON STANDARD (IOWA)

"Hilarious!"
—TEENA JONES
THE TEENA JONES SHOW, KMSR-AM (DALLAS)

HOW TO SURVIVE YOUR MOVE

"After 14 moves in 34 years, I thought I knew everything about how to move. But I was wrong—I could have used this book in every stage of my life in moving."
—CAREN MASEM, GREENSBORO, NORTH CAROLINA

"This is a good resource book for do-it-yourself movers to learn some of the best tips in making a move easier."
—JOANNE FRIED, U-HAUL INTERNATIONAL, INC.

HOW TO SURVIVE YOUR MARRIAGE

"Reader-friendly and packed full of good advice. They should hand this out at the marriage license counter!"

—BOB NACHSHIN, CELEBRITY DIVORCE ATTORNEY AND CO-AUTHOR OF
I DO, YOU DO . . . BUT JUST SIGN HERE

"Full of honest advice from newlyweds and longtime couples. This book answers the question–'How do other people do it?'"

—ELLEN SABIN, M.P.H., M.P.A.
EXECUTIVE DIRECTOR, EQUALITY IN MARRIAGE INSTITUTE

"This book is the best wedding present I received! It's great to go into a marriage armed with the advice of hundreds of people who have been through it all already."

—ANN MEAGHER, NEWLYWED

HOW TO SURVIVE YOUR BABY'S FIRST YEAR

"An amazing kaleidoscope of insights into surviving parenthood, this book will reassure moms and dads that they are not alone in the often scary world of bringing up baby."

—JOSEF SOLOWAY, M.D., F.A.A.P.
CLINICAL ASSOCIATE PROFESSOR OF PEDIATRICS
WEILL MEDICAL COLLEGE OF CORNELL UNIVERSITY

"Full of real-life ideas and tips. If you love superb resource books for being the best parent you can be, you'll love *How to Survive Your Baby's First Year.*"

—ERIN BROWN CONROY, M.A.
AUTHOR, COLUMNIST, MOTHER OF TWELVE, AND CREATOR OF TOTALLYFITMOM.COM

"The HUNDREDS OF HEADS folks have done it again! Literally hundreds of moms and dads from all over offer their nuggets of wisdom—some sweet, some funny, all smart—on giving birth, coming home and bringing up baby."

—ANDREA SARVADY
AUTHOR OF BABY GAMI

How to
Survive
Your
Teenager

WARNING:

This guide contains differing
opinions. Hundreds of heads
will not always agree.
Advice taken in combination may
cause unwanted side effects. Use
your head when selecting advice.

How to
Survive
Your
Teenager

by Hundreds of Still-Sane Parents Who Did*   *and some things to avoid, from a few whose kids drove them nuts™

edited by
BETH REINGOLD GLUCK AND JOEL ROSENFELD

Hundreds of Heads Books, Inc.
ATLANTA

Illustrations © 2005 by Image Club
Cover photograph by PictureQuest

Cover and book design by Elizabeth Johnsboen

See page 234-235 for credits and permissions.

How to survive your teenager: by hundreds of still-sane parents who did and some things to avoid from a few whose kids drove them nuts / edited by Beth Gluck and Joel Rosenfeld.
    p.cm.
ISBN 0-9746292-3-5
1. Parent and teenager. 2. Parenting. I. Gluck, Beth, 1958- II. Rosenfeld, Joel, 1957-
HQ799.15.H67 2005
    649'.125--dc22   2005003030

HUNDREDS OF HEADS BOOKS, INC.
#230
2221 Peachtree Road, Suite D
Atlanta, Georgia 30309

ISBN 0-9746292-3-5

Printed in U.S.A.
10 9 8 7 6 5 4 3 2 1

CONTENTS

Introduction

The world contains well over a billion people between the ages of 12 and 20. That's enough to fill a small planet: in fact, many of them seem to *come* from another planet. True, only a small fraction of these teens are your direct responsibility here on earth. But, as you've no doubt discovered, they carry with them an entire universe of problems, dramas, issues, feelings, and MP3 files.

And for those teens you do claim as your own, from the first slammed door to the last temper tantrum, from their first pimple to their last day living at home, it's your job to get them through it alive and survive the experience yourself. If you're one of those reach-for-the-moon types, you might also be aiming to raise your teens to be upstanding members of society.

Don't attempt to navigate these treacherous waters alone. This book, the sixth in the HUNDREDS OF HEADS™ Survival Guide series, grew out of the simple idea that when you're facing any of life's major challenges, it's good to get advice from those who have gone before you. Other advice books, no matter how smart or expert their authors, are generally limited to the knowledge of only one or two people. This book takes a different approach: It compiles the advice of *hundreds* of parents who successfully raised a teenager or two and emerged with some wisdom to share. If two heads are better than one, as the saying goes, then hundreds of them should be even better.

Among the many bits of wisdom here, you'll learn at least one way to keep your teen from slamming the bedroom door. You'll discover the best places to teach your teen to drive. You'll learn what to say if they happen to crash the family car through the back of the garage, or come home with purple hair, or tell you they're sexually active. You'll read about a unique way to get them to go to class, and perhaps even excel in their studies. You'll find out how to talk to your teen about the most difficult issues, and actually get a response.

You'll also notice that parents have different methods for getting the most out of their teen, and that not all parents agree on the right method. Here you can read all points of view: It's up to you to decide which approach works for you.

Most of all, you'll understand that you are not alone. Reading *How to Survive Your Teenager* is like inviting hundreds of your friends and neighbors over for coffee and conversation on a very important topic.

It's been said that the teen years are the final and most difficult challenge of parenthood; the dissertation for your Ph.D. in Parenting. If that's the case, consider this your ultimate textbook and you can relax about the final exam.

BETH REINGOLD GLUCK
JOEL ROSENFELD

KEY

So you'll know just how expert our respondents really are, we've included their credentials in this book. Look for these icons:

    ☻ = a son
    🐾 = a daughter
    Numbers refer to ages of children

Brave New World: Entering the Teen Years

What happened? One moment, you're having a great time with your child, who looks so cute and smart and lovable. The next moment, you're informed by an awkward-looking alien that everything is your fault. Then the door slams. Congratulations: You are now the parent of a teenager. We'd like to say it's an easy ride, but it's not. Hang on, and learn from others who share the first moments of life with a teenager.

MY HUSBAND AND I MADE IT THROUGH the diaper stage, the terrible twos, the toddler years, and kindergarten with each of our four kids. But nothing prepared us for the most challenging parenting obstacle: the teenage years.

—JERENE
WILLIAMSPORT, PENNSYLVANIA
👶13 👶12 👶7 👶7

IF SOMEONE HAD TOLD ME WHAT A TEENAGER WAS LIKE, I WOULD HAVE PASSED.

—ARION MILLET
WATERVLIET, MICHIGAN
👶15 👶12

Talk to parents of older kids who are now wonderful and productive adults. They will regale you with stories of how horrid their teens once were.

—*C.W.*
BOULDER,
COLORADO
22

NOT ALL TEENAGERS HAVE TO BE TROUBLED—or trouble for the parents. When I picture one of my daughters as a teenager, I just see her hanging around with her friends, laughing. Don't assume that your teenager will be difficult or unhappy.

—*JACK MORRIS*
WALTHAM, MASSACHUSETTS
42 41 36

· · · · · · · ·

I FIRST REALIZED TEENS WERE NOW LIVING under my roof when the phone started to ring more often and the rooms got messier. As soon as they were teenagers, they didn't know how to hang up clothes. Everything was on the floor!

—*RHONDA SYRTASH*
THORNHILL, ONTARIO, CANADA
21 17 17

· · · · · · · ·

IT WAS OBVIOUS MY KID WAS A TEEN because of the change in attitude and the secrecy. Teens are trying to become independent and they start to pull away by not sharing every little thing and by questioning your authority. The trick is to teach them to be independent and respectful. And when you master this, please let me know!

—*KIMERA BROWN*
CLEVELAND, OHIO

· · · · · · · ·

HE ANSWERS THE PHONE and everyone thinks it's me. The bedroom door is closed and locked all the time. He wears Band-Aids on his face to cover the pimples. And he wears the uniform—the cap with the bill squished in, and his pants start slipping down lower so you can see the boxers.

—*DAN B.*
ATLANTA, GEORGIA
14 12 5

LATE ONE NIGHT, MY SON HAD A NIGHTMARE and called out. I woke up, ran down the hall, opened his door, and screamed: I saw the shadow of a man standing by his bed. My husband came running down the hall, asking, "What's the matter?" I said, "There's a man in his room!" My husband turned on the light: It was my son! In my mind he was still a child. It really took me by surprise.

> —*CAREN MASEM*
> *GREENSBORO, NORTH CAROLINA*
> 😊 *33* 😊 *28*

. . . .

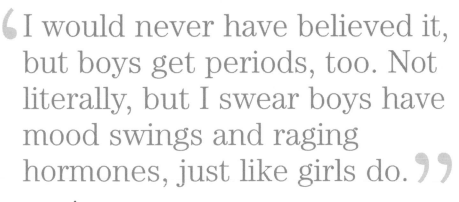

❝ I would never have believed it, but boys get periods, too. Not literally, but I swear boys have mood swings and raging hormones, just like girls do. ❞

> —*ANONYMOUS*
> *PHILADELPHIA, PENNSYLVANIA*
> 😊 *13* 😊 *12*

. . . .

TRY TO BECOME INDEPENDENTLY WEALTHY so you don't have to do anything else when they hit their teens. Young children require more time, but the demands of a teenager put more stress on you because they're more difficult to meet. A toddler wants food, attention, and some basic needs met. A teenager wants all that *plus* independence, and that's hard to give. *Plus* endless transportation.

> —*MICHAEL WHITE*
> *GLENDORA, CALIFORNIA*
> 😊 *20* 😊 *18* 😊 *17* 😊 *15* 😊 *13* 😊 *10* 😊 *6*

OUR FIRST TWO TEENAGERS ARE GIRLS, so yes, they are moody, and I am convinced it is hormones. If you are going to get upset over moodiness or being talked back to, you are going to have a long road. Humor can defuse any situation. And remember, the heat of the moment is not the best time to talk to your kids. Realize you can come back to an issue when everyone is cooler.

—*L.C.*
YARMOUTH, MAINE
👧 16 👧 14 👶 11

• • • • • • • •

THERE IS *NO* PAYBACK. They are selfish, bratty, and provide no pleasure. I am not sure what happened: I keep trying different things. She is surviving and I am drowning. I want connection and she wants to run. I get a smile only when I give her money. I cannot *afford* a very happy relationship with her.

—*ARION MILLET*
WATERVLIET, MICHIGAN
👧 15 👧 12

TIPS FOR GETTING ALONG WITH YOUR TEENAGER

#1: Try to offer advice based on personal experiences without seeming like the all-knowing adult.

#2: Spend quality time with your teenager. Do not just give them money to entertain themselves.

—*JULIE G., CHURCH YOUTH GROUP MENTOR*
OKLAHOMA CITY, OKLAHOMA

BUY DEODORANT AND ZIT CREAM. My son needs both, but he hates to buy them because it's embarrassing. My way of handling his disappointment about zits and body odor is to tell him that he inherited it, and like his dad and I did, he'll get through it—well, the zits, at least.

—*NANCY
LEE, MASSACHUSETTS*

· · · · · · · ·

"Teenager" and "narcissism" —they're synonymous.

—*S. STEWART
SAN FRANCISCO,
CALIFORNIA*

GIRLS AND BOYS ARE VERY DIFFERENT. Girls tell their mothers everything! Friends of mine with girls told me it was like going through adolescence again with their daughters; all that pain, all that suffering. Boys, on the other hand, tell their mothers nothing; that's very painful, too. It's pain either way. One of my dear friends, with a daughter, remarked that it takes a lot of courage to be a mother.

—*S.S.
SARATOGA SPRINGS, NEW YORK
22*

· · · · · · · ·

BEFORE I SAW IT COMING, my son hit his teens—hormones in sneakers, with a sense of immortality. I enjoyed waking him up at the crack of noon every weekend. I knew he was a teenager when we played a new game in his room called "Find the floor." Fashion became a one-word oxymoron. Baggy pants, $100 sneakers, and a T-shirt that always featured some odd message. His appetite *exploded*. Actually, I think I gained weight watching him eat! He just pounded it down, and never got fat. When he moved away to college, I did not lose a son: I gained a refrigerator!

—*BOB FITZSIMMONS*

UNDERSTAND THAT IT'S A SHORT PERIOD IN LIFE, so don't deny them this period. They are only testing the waters of life. However, you do need to have life jackets on hand for them and yourself.

—*J.P.*
DAVENPORT, IOWA
👧 *28* 👧 *25* 👧 *22*

• • • • • • • •

IT'S HARDER TO GET A GIRL THROUGH the teenage years than a boy. You have a sweet little girl and suddenly this lurking, teenage horror will pop out, probably when something traumatic is happening in your own life. My daughter and I would have a fight about something inconsequential and suddenly she was leaping up from the dinner table and finding the nearest door to slam. Then she wouldn't speak to me for days at a time and I was left wondering why. They will outgrow this: the problem is, you never quite remember that while it's happening.

—*SHARON LONDON*
SAN FRANCISCO, CALIFORNIA
👧 *43* 👧 *40*

• • • • • • • •

I DON'T THINK MANY PARENTS REALIZE just how hard middle school is, primarily for girls. Girls can really change when they get to sixth, seventh and eighth grades. One of the girls my 14-year-old thought was a friend started telling everyone what a "loser" she thought my daughter was— really spelling it out. As much as she knew this girl was just being hurtful, I could tell she felt there must be something wrong with her for this girl to say that. We did what we could to improve her self-esteem.

—*ANONYMOUS*
NEW JERSEY
👧 *17* 👧 *14*

YOU WILL NOT BELIEVE THAT THIS IS the same sweet child of just a few years back. They are moody, don't like anything you say, don't like how you look, don't like how you talk, or anything about you.

—*PATTY LAMBROPOULOS*
CHICAGO, ILLINOIS
23 21 17 14

· · · · · · · ·

'If something doesn't work out my daughter's way, we get the rolling of her eyes. I'm sure it will get worse before it gets better.'

—*RICK BARBERO*
GAITHERSBURG, MARYLAND
12 5

· · · · · · · ·

FOR WHATEVER REASON SOME KIDS seem to reach puberty and then forget all about taking care of their personal appearance. This usually happens with boys, but with me it was my daughter. I really don't know why this happens but other parents have told me it happened with their kids, too. My daughter would wear stuff over and over without bothering to wash it. Some of her socks could have stood up by themselves; it was disgusting. I think kids just have so much to deal with while going through puberty that taking care of things like that doesn't seem important. But I insisted that she take the time to do laundry and look presentable.

—*REILLY BURTON*
SWISSVALE, PENNSYLVANIA
16

IGNORE THE SMALL STUFF

All of a sudden they view you as a nerdy alien from the bottom of the earth. They become so consumed by their own life that they can't see beyond it, and they can't see a parent as a normal person. At first I expected the same things from them that I had expected in their early childhood, but that didn't work. I ended up hounding them to do things, like clean up their rooms or get certain chores done. Communication became nonexistent, and that was frustrating. Teenagers are at such a vulnerable place and they are doing the best they can to deal with stuff. I decided I'd rather  have some communication with them than none, because then I'd have some influence and be able to guide them. If we had a totally adversarial relationship, I wouldn't have those opportunities. So I gave up hounding them: I picked my battles. That made things easier, not only for them, but also for me. I began to enjoy my children again.

—Jo E. Shea
Parkdale, Oregon
23 21 19

LATELY, MY SON HAS BEEN GROWING like it's his job. He's five feet seven and he gained about six inches in the last six months. It's ridiculous; we'll buy clothes for him and he'll outgrow them in a week. The poor boy is all elbows and feet right now. He just gets used to how his body works and then it changes again and he's tripping over his own feet. How should parents deal with growth spurts? By smiling a lot and not yelling at them when they fumble a plate or a cup. Remind them that eventually they *will* stop growing and get comfortable in their own skin. Don't make a big deal about them tripping over their own feet; they're self-conscious enough now anyway.

—*ANGELA FLATHERS-HENNESSEY*
DEWITT, IOWA
🙂12 🙂7

• • • • • • • • •

I KNEW I WAS LIVING WITH TEENAGERS when I started talking to them through the crack of their doors and when they started getting up at the crack of noon. My 15-year-old's appetite is so crazy that after we go food shopping he just sticks a straw in the refrigerator door and sucks everything out in one slurp! Half an hour later, he's complaining that there's nothing to eat in this house.

—*PAMELA BODLEY*
YONKERS, NEW YORK

• • • • • • • •

Try to remember when you were a teen.

—*D.D.*
DARLINGTON,
MARYLAND
👧33 🙂31

MY SON STARTED VOLUNTEERING to take a bath. Before, I had to nag him day after day to take care of himself. But once his view on girls started to change he suddenly became an expert on which soaps we should be buying and which shampoos worked best.

—*LARRY FELBING*
POLAND, OHIO
🙂24

THEY'RE SO EXPENSIVE!

Middle-income families spend between $9,390 and $9,530 per year on the typical teenager.

LIVING WITH TEENAGERS IS LIKE living with a bomb that could go off at any minute. And when it goes off, don't for a second think it's done with. It'll go off again and again. They're hormonally victimized and very mercurial. It's the teenage version of being a tantrum-throwing toddler. The best response is no different than it was when they were two-year-olds pitching a fit: Walk away unimpressed. If the episode requires a time-out, punishment, or a flat-out "No," do it.

—*JOHN W.*
LONGMEADOW, MASSACHUSETTS

• • • • • • • •

I THINK IT'S HARDER WITH GIRLS because they are pushing against you, but they still want to please you. They struggle constantly with those two desires. But with boys it's different: They push against you, but they don't care so much about pleasing.

—*ANONYMOUS*
LONG VALLEY, NEW JERSEY
👧 *32* 👦 *23*

• • • • • • • •

ONE OF MY ONE DAUGHTERS put all her tomboy gear away. It was the same time she started taking more interest in her appearance, including asking me about the virtues of makeup. She also  started hanging around more with her girl friends instead of playing baseball or basketball with the boys. Her wardrobe got completely revamped. Gone were the T-shirts and jeans and in their place were blouses and skirts. For a while I thought a new kid had moved into my house.

—*JANE YASKO*
BOARDMAN, OHIO
👧 *22* 👧 *22*

LOWER THOSE EXPECTATIONS

One day out of the blue (or so it seemed to us) our happy, sweet, little boy turned into one of those sullen, withdrawn creatures that we saw lying around other people's houses. Being convinced of our superior parenting skills, we were stunned that "it"—this menacing, teenage/monster metamorphosis thing— actually happened to us. Suddenly, our "lines of communication" were clogged with grunts, glares and shouts. Friends tried to bolster our spirits by telling us that we shouldn't despair, the Martians who have stolen our son's brain will return it in five years. "It will pass," others said. "He'll have to talk when he wants the car keys." Devastated, we signed up for a support group for parents going through the same trauma. I'll never forget when the leader listened patiently to my list of complaints about our son locking himself in his room, boycotting family dinners, and refusing to come to visit. She asked us, "Does he go to school?" "Yes," we said. "Does he take drugs?" she continued. "No." "Does he like girls?" "Yes." "Go home," she said, "You've got a good kid. The problem is your expectations. The secret to successful survival of the teenage years is to lower your expectations." We've since modified that philosophy to "have no expectations," and can report much smoother sailing with our other two kids entering the danger zone.

　　—*ANONYMOUS*
　　CHARLESTON, SOUTH CAROLINA
　　😊18 😊15 😊12 😊2

I KNEW MY DAUGHTER WAS A TEENAGER when she turned 15. Up until then we'd been very close, but suddenly one day she came home and she didn't like me anymore. That was tough. A good friend's advice helped a lot. She said, "This is not personal." It felt very personal, but I held on to that thought. Another thing that helped is that my daughter said to me, "Mom, you need to get a life." I realized that she was right, so instead of focusing so much on her, I began focusing on things I wanted to do for me.

—*LAURIE C.*
SAN DIEGO, CALIFORNIA

• • • • • • • •

❝The worst thing about dealing with teenagers is the moodiness, aside from the fact that you're nervous all the time.❞

—*ANONYMOUS*
CHICAGO, ILLINOIS
24 20 19 17 15

• • • • • • • •

TO MY CHILDREN I'M DUMBER THAN A ROCK. They challenge everything I say: "No it's not!" they say. "Yeah, it is," I say. "You wanna bet?" they say. There are times I'm done being so stupid, so I tell them, "I really apologize that you've got such a stupid parent." It catches them off guard. They step back and say, "I didn't mean it that way." It helps them realize that they're making it seem like I'm dumb.

—*CHERYL NORTON*
WASHOUGAL, WASHINGTON
13

HE SUDDENLY KNEW MORE THAN I DID about just about everything. Practically overnight he went from viewing me as the one with all the answers to viewing me as someone who knew nothing. He, on the other hand, became an expert on just about everything: No matter what the subject was he was right and I was wrong. I remember one time that he insisted the back bedroom in the house was considerably colder than the one in front. One day I came home with thermometers and put them in the two rooms. They showed what I knew they would: the rooms were the same. He accused me of doctoring them! Ain't the teenage years grand?

—C.C.
POLAND, OHIO
🌼25 🌼21

Prayer is the only answer!

—PEGGY
SEATTLE,
WASHINGTON
🐾10

. . . .

MY DAUGHTER IS 11, on the cusp of her teen years. But I have to say, I'm not dreading the teens nearly as much as most moms I know. That's because we have a very close relationship. We sit together every night at supper and talk— no TV allowed. She tells me everything, who her friends are, which boys she likes, and even when she misbehaves. Although I know part of the reason she tells me everything is that she loves to shock me, I'm careful to show my surprise, but not overreact and scare her from telling me things in the future. My biggest fear is that my daughter will stop telling me important things about her life. I know that as she gets older, she may not tell me *everything*, but I want her to know that she *can* tell me everything if she wants to.

—ANONYMOUS
ALLENTOWN, PENNSYLVANIA
🐾11

THE "MOM" TOUR

When I found myself losing communication with my 14-year-old son, I knew that it was just the beginning: Not so much that my son was entering into adolescence, but that I was getting old. I found myself trying to figure out where the last 14 years had gone. Looking in the mirror, it was obvious they had gone south. I found myself feeling depressed when I realized my son could survive seeing me a total of five minutes a day. That's about one minute five times a day, asking for permission to go out on the weekend, asking for a few bucks. And that's if I got lucky to have the honor of a total of five minutes. He could actually live in his room, I thought. As long as he had his guitar, the Internet, and a phone, I was of no use.

It took a while to figure out how I could bring us closer again. I found myself at Ticketmaster, searching for concert dates on all bands I knew he liked. I bought three tickets—for my son, for myself, and for any friend he wanted to bring. It was the "Pop Disaster Tour"—Green Day, Blink 182, and Jimmy Eat World. Wow! Not only did he think I was the coolest mom, I had an awesome time. I even met some fathers who were chaperoning their kids. Little by little, and concert after concert, we grew closer than even before. But best of all, I found myself again. It's sad how we get caught up in the complexities of what is called real life and forget who we were, back when we were really feeling alive. I've even got him playing Led Zeppelin and the Beatles, and the satisfaction in his face when he knows he's playing my stuff is incredible. Sometimes I just lie on his bed playing "Pac-Man" on his game system while he plays Cheap Trick, and nobody could tell me I'm not 14 again.

If you can't beat 'em, join 'em. You'll have the time of your life.

—*Cecilia Valdes-Shaw*
Coral Gables, Florida
14

IF YOU'RE GOING TO HAVE KIDS, don't have girls; they're just difficult as hell as teenagers. My daughter at age 15, slipped out of the house at 2 a.m. We found her gone and called the police. She was with two boys and they were drinking beer. We raised hell, and we made sure she couldn't get out the back door again. Now it's a family story, but at the time it was the worst thing that happened to us.

—*ANONYMOUS*
   SARASOTA, FLORIDA
   🐶 41 🐶 40 😊 38 😊 37 😊 36

• • • • • • • •

YOU KNOW YOUR CHILD HAS BECOME A TEENAGER when he suddenly starts challenging your authority. Suddenly, he wants to know *why* he has to do something instead of just obeying.

—*KARI GOERKE*
   CENTENNIAL, COLORADO
   😊 14 😊 11

• • • • • • • •

SUDDENLY YOU, THE PARENT, are no longer important. Their friends become important. And you can be as open with them as you want, but they will hide things from you. My daughter was pretty open with a lot of things. At 15, all of a sudden boys would start coming over and hanging on every word she said. She was pretty open with what was going on—her friends having sex and all that. But then she closed off and wouldn't allow me to know things. When she turned 16, she started hiding things and sneaking out of the house. All you can do is hope that all those things you taught them in the years before will remain in their head; and you can't be so strict because then they'll rebel totally.

—*PAT WILLIAMS*
   ATLANTA, GEORGIA
   🐶 21 😊 19

Teenagers aren't easy to be around. They're agitating because they're agitated. They're in a stage when their bodies don't fit, their minds don't fit, and all they want to do is fit in.

—*KATE*
   ALFORD,
   MASSACHUSETTS

I remember what my older sister told me when my daughter turned 13: "From now on," she said, "everything is your fault."

—*N.*
BROOKLYN,
NEW YORK
17

IT'S USEFUL TO REMEMBER how much of adolescence is hormonally fueled. You can't expect teens to behave rationally. The hard thing is, they're not consistently bad or good—it's all over the place. My daughter will run up and hug me while I'm still stinging from the spat we had 10 minutes earlier.

—*VERONICA LORSON FOWLER*
AMES, IOWA
17 14 7

• • • • • • • •

THE PHYSICAL CHANGES ARE A DIFFICULT THING for a boy. He was in a play and he was the lead and his voice was at the peak of changing. It was really rough, but he pulled it off. I told him, "Everyone goes through it, so don't be self-conscious about it."

—*DANIEL BERMAN*
ATLANTA, GEORGIA
14 12 5

Domestic Politics: Getting Along at Home

It was once your home. Now there's an occupying army bivouacked in your bathroom. Dinnertime could be a sitcom episode in perpetual rerun. Your phone is not your phone. Neither is your TV. Neither is all the food that was once in your refrigerator. And the city has flagged your teen's room for environmental cleanup. It's safe to say that change is in order. Here are some stories and tips on retaking what was once yours—or, at least surviving until your teen moves out.

I DON'T THINK I'VE EVER MET A LOGICAL TEENAGER. I've met a lot of smart teenagers but not logical ones. The teenage mind doesn't think that way. It's like living with a houseful of hormones; they're so volatile.

—*CAREN MASEM*
GREENSBORO, NORTH CAROLINA
🌀*33* 🌀*28*

THE MOST IMPORTANT THING YOU CAN DO IN RAISING A TEENAGER IS TO INVEST YOUR TIME WITH THEM.

—*S.C.*
FT. SMITH, ARIZONA
🌀*18* 🌀*12*

BETWEEN MY JOB, MY HUSBAND'S JOB, and our boys' various sporting events, we led a crazy, hectic life. To ensure family bonding didn't get lost in the shuffle, we always waited to have dinner until the last person's function was finished for the day. For example, if their father was working late, the boys came home from practice, grabbed a small snack and did all of their homework before we ate. The rearranging was worth it: we bonded a lot during that one meal together each day.

> —JOAN K. HITCHENS
> CENTENNIAL, COLORADO
> 😊 32 😊 28

• • • • • • • •

IF YOU WANT YOUR TEENS TO TURN OUT all right, you have to be prepared to give up a lot. I was always at home with them. So many mothers work and then give them too many things. We were not overly indulgent but we took an interest in our family. We've been very lucky in our children.

> —K.F.
> CUPAR, FIFE, SCOTLAND
> 39 34 31

• • • • • • • •

WHEN I WANT HER TO GET OFF THE PHONE, I pretend that I have to make a phone call and ask her to bring the cordless phone to me. I refuse to buy her a cell phone or put in a second line, but I have to have call-waiting or I would miss too many other calls! Also, set the kitchen timer on the stove when you need to limit her talk time. The loud annoying noise lets everyone know it's time for her to hang up. Her little sister especially gets a kick out of this!

> —KIMERA BROWN
> CLEVELAND, OHIO

> Whatever
> works with
> toddlers works
> with teens,
> except physical
> restraints.
>
> —K.S.
> SEATTLE,
> WASHINGTON
> 33 32

IF YOU CAN PLAY GAMES WITH YOUR KIDS, it's great. We also take them to dinner and a movie. My kids would just as soon go with us to the movies. When they go with us, we pay: Without us, they pay.

—*KAREN*
KNOXVILLE, TENNESSEE
🌝 *17* 🌝 *14*

• • • • • • • •

❝ We talked a lot and went to places like museums and cafés together. Sometimes I went places with them that I wasn't interested in at all like a basket-ball game. But I just smiled and chose to enjoy myself. I didn't care about basketball, but I cared about spending time with my son and daughter. ❞

—*M.S.L.*
WAIKOLOA, HAWAII
🌝 *40* 🌝 *37*

• • • • • • • •

WHEN YOU COME FROM A GOOD HOME, there's no way you won't be a good person. Family is more important than anything. It's more important than money.

—*BATIA ELKAYAM*
LOS ANGELES, CALIFORNIA
🌝 🌝

I wish I hadn't given my son his own TV. The family time lost was not worth the convenience.

—*S.S.*
SARATOGA SPRINGS, NEW YORK
22

PUT DOWN THE DUST RAG AND GET INVOLVED in their lives. I spent my whole life thinking that my house had to be perfect: neat and clean, everything in its place. I worked full time, too. I missed so much of my kids' lives that way. Enjoy them while you can; before you know it, they'll be turning 40.

—*C.S.*
CAPE MAY, NEW JERSEY
39 37 34 32

• • • • • • • •

I WISH I COULD CHANGE my son's sleeping habits. Kids that age stay up all hours of the night and then sleep until noon, and that doesn't jibe with the way anybody else in the house lives. On weekends or in the summertime I'll be eating lunch and he'll still be in bed. And then when I'm trying to get some sleep he's playing PlayStation until two in the morning. That's just not right.

—*M.B.*
CRANBERRY TOWNSHIP, PENNSYLVANIA
18

• • • • • • • •

MY DAUGHTER HAS ALWAYS ENJOYED FOOD. She is well within the healthy height/weight range, but she favors music over sports and may not get as much exercise as she should. My husband and I never discussed weight with my daughter, and never commented in any way negatively. What we do say is that if one eats healthy and gets moderate exercise, the shape you have is the one God gave you. While my child has issues with her figure at times (especially as so many girls at her school are painfully thin), we try to help her put this in the context of other positive features.

—*BRENDA KILGORE*
PHOENIX, CANBERRA, AUSTRALIAN CAPITAL TERRITORY, AUSTRALIA
15

MORE THAN A MAKEOVER

My son loves interior design. I had an ancient Singer sewing machine and Allen started using it to sew patches on all his clothes. Then he looked at the family room and said, "Mom, you know, this room needs some work; we ought to fix it up." I had deadlines and things to do and places to go, but I realized that if I didn't do things with him now, when was I going to do them? He was so into redecorating and he wanted to do it with me! You hear stories about how when teenagers get their first car, they're gone, but Allen wanted to get in his car and go down to the fabric store!

The first thing he wanted to do was paint the sofa. My first reaction was "No, wait, I paid $700 for that sofa!" But instead I said, "How would you paint it?" We ended up buying a gallon of gesso and turning the sides and back of the sofa into a canvas, which we then decorated with a Greek-key stencil. You can't paint the cushions, of course, so we had to slipcover them. We bought some beige denim and Allen sewed the slipcovers. We ended up redoing the entire room in a Greek theme, and that became his entertainment room. His friends thought the room was totally cool.

My son is grown and married now, and the family room needs redoing, but I hesitate because it reminds me of a special time spent exploring my son's talents and creativity.

—D.W.
SAN DIEGO, CALIFORNIA

I only go into her room to retrieve dirty dishes and glassware; otherwise, the rest of the family would eventually be reduced to using paper plates and cups.

—*N.*
BROOKLYN,
NEW YORK
17

IF YOU'RE LIKE ME, you probably buy a lot of low-fat foods. But when your teenage boy starts eating you out of house and home, a little fat can help. It fills them up faster and gives them extra calories, which they apparently need. We bought full-fat milk, yogurt, sour cream, and mayo. Lots of cheese! We encourage them to put cheese and mayo on their sandwiches and wash it all down with full-fat milk followed by full-fat ice cream.

—*TONY*
CHICAGO, ILLINOIS
17 15

• • • • • • • •

TEENS LOVE CONVENIENCE. If you have healthy foods ready to go, like good leftovers ready to nuke and healthy snacks, they really will eat them. When we finally stopped buying the junky convenience foods and had nothing in the house but healthier choices, that's what our kids started eating.

—*MISSY*
DETROIT, MICHIGAN
14 12 9

• • • • • • • •

A LITTLE MODERATION MIGHT BE BETTER than strict rules when it comes to teenagers and eating. My daughter doesn't have rules about what she can and can't eat. If she chooses pizza over broiled chicken or chocolate s'mores over fresh fruit, we tell ourselves that eventually she'll realize healthy choices make healthy bodies. In contrast, one of her best friend's parents have hard-and-fast food rules. That girl gets little pizza and no chocolate treats at her house. What her parents don't know is that the last time she spent the night at our house, she drank three Sprites before breakfast.

—*ANONYMOUS*
DENVER, COLORADO
13

FOR A WHILE MY DAUGHTER was doing too much snacking, but she put on weight and decided to eat more sensibly. Now she is very pleased with herself. I think the extra snacking came with the ups and downs of dealing with teen-related issues. I found that the best way to handle it was to let her handle it herself. She felt especially good about her success because she brought it about all by herself.

—*B.S.K.*
SEATTLE, WASHINGTON
🐕 16

• • • • • • • •

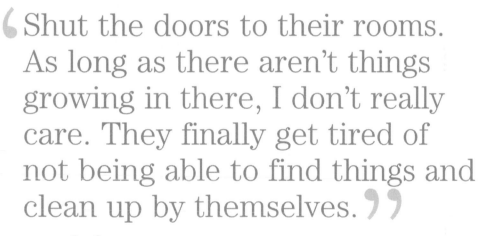

'Shut the doors to their rooms. As long as there aren't things growing in there, I don't really care. They finally get tired of not being able to find things and clean up by themselves. '

—*PAT CURRY*
ATHENS, GEORGIA
🐕 17 🐕 15

• • • • • • • •

MY DAUGHTER HAS BETTER EATING HABITS than I do and sets a good example for me. She is thin and likes herself that way and her eating habits are improving as she gets older. She is learning to cook and makes a wonderful meatloaf. She loves fruit and vegetables and doesn't eat a lot of junk food; no cookies, ice cream, donuts, or candy.

—*CATHY FRANKLIN*
PURVIS, MISSISSIPPI
🐕 17

SIDE BY SIDE

You always have all these fantasies of how bonding with your kids is going to be, like you see yourself camping or fishing happily with them, or something like that. But your kid may turn out to be someone very different than you, and different than you imagined. If you try to force them to conform to your fantasy you're going to end up with sullen, bored kids at that camping trip. A lot of parents with sullen teenagers fail to see that the kid has to matter as much in the equation as they do. Find out what they like to do, then base your bonding time around that. My son is into music, so I take him to shows, or to a music store in another town that he couldn't get to by himself. I'd rather spend my day hiking, but it needs to be about him. If I do these things with him I get a better understanding of who he is, I'm not baffled when he mentions the most recent obscure band he's into. It's hard, I know, when you work hard, to spend your free time doing things with your kids that seem silly to you. But the same is true of them. They go to school, they don't want to spend their weekend camping if there's a concert they'd rather go to. You have to compromise. I hope that by the time my son realizes camping might be fun we'll be good enough friends that he'll still want to do it with me.

—PETER STEUR
BRISBANE, QUEENSLAND, AUSTRALIA
24 21 14

WHEN YOU'RE WRESTLING AROUND with your teenage son for fun, make sure you win. Subconsciously he's testing you to make sure you're still the king of the house. If you can't beat him by brute strength, fight dirty—bite, scratch, take a well-placed shot—anything it takes to win.

—*JOHN COOKE*
GREELEY, COLORADO
23 21

· · · · · · · ·

WE REARED THE BOYS IN THE SOUTHEASTERN U.S. where vegetables are summer staples. I believe in good cooking, and several times a week, we fix full-course meals with all appropriate food groups. We always have fruit in the house and we taught them to drink milk and juice more often than soft drinks. They have their weaknesses, such as McDonalds and Pizza Hut, but moderation is the key. Not one is overweight, and they all watch the scales, except the youngest, who could add a few pounds.

—*C. HOPE CLARK*
PHOENIX, ARIZONA
31 26 21 19

· · · · · · · ·

FIX BALANCED MEALS, instead of picking up everything from McDonalds. I always tried to have something green on the table every day, along with some starch, some milk, and some protein. Of course, despite your best efforts, you can't control everything. When my daughter was 16, she got a job at the grocery store and suddenly wasn't home in the evenings. I later found out she'd been eating a dozen donuts for dinner, which contributed to a 20-pound weight gain.

—*LUCIA BOLES*
ST. LOUIS, MISSOURI
53 52

Keep them involved in activities—sports, dance, that kind of thing—so that they have an outlet for their feelings.

—*PAT WILLIAMS*
ATLANTA, GEORGIA
21 19

His answer to everything is "I know, I know." I say, "You have to empty the dishwasher." He says, "I know, I know." I say, "Obviously you didn't know because I had to tell you." And he says, "I know."

—*D.B.*
ATLANTA, GEORGIA
👦14 👦12 👦5

I HAVE THREE TEENAGE BOYS and they are literally eating my wife and me out of house and home. It's incredible how much those boys can eat. I know three girls of the same ages would not be eating like this. They never seem to be full. It's amazing.

—*STEVE O'HODNICK*
SWISSVALE, PENNSYLVANIA
👦18 👦16 👦13

• • • • • • • •

OUR GIRLS FIGHT ABOUT CLOTHES. One's always taking something out of the other one's closet, and it's usually an item that hasn't been worn for months —but as soon as the one who's been "taken from" sees that item of clothing, she's screaming, "Give that back to me! That's my favorite shirt!"

—*WILLIAM SMITH*
SAN FRANCISCO, CALIFORNIA
👧23 👧21 👦16

• • • • • • • •

IT'S IMPORTANT FOR PARENTS TO REALIZE that eating habits do change. Teens don't eat like children or like adults: they need more frequent, smaller meals, around five a day. My kids like healthy food; sushi, pizza, and sandwiches rather than fries and hamburgers. I also encouraged them to cook their own meals.

—*DEVORAH STONE*
VICTORIA, BRITISH COLUMBIA, CANADA
👧22 👧19 👦12

NO PRYING EYES

Don't snoop: Parents have to respect their teenagers' privacy. I know lots of mothers who read their kids' diaries and listen in on their phone calls. "You have to know what your kids are doing," they insist. I've never snooped on my kids. I believe that if you build a good relationship with your kids, they'll be more honest with you and you won't have to snoop. My daughter had always been a respectful kid. But when she turned 14 or 15, she started hanging around with kids I didn't care for. She started to change. I thought she had gotten involved with drugs or sex. I wanted to snoop, but I didn't. Instead, I let her bring those friends over to our house so I could observe them. Finally I found out what was going on. My daughter started to confide in me that she had started to try booze and, almost, drugs. Slowly, she eased away from those friends, and she started acting more like her old self. I believe to this day that if I would have snooped and betrayed her trust, she would never have told me anything.

—W.F.
MERTZTOWN, PENNSYLVANIA
24   20

WHY YOU JUST CAN'T GET THEM OUT OF BED

Adolescents need about nine hours of sleep for optimal functioning. During the week, most don't get that much.

BOTH OF MY GIRLS DECIDED to become vegetarians at age 13 or 14. I am a carnivore, so it was hard at first to make sure they got well-balanced meals. But I adjusted. They are both healthy and slim: we must be doing it right.

—HEIDE A.W. KAMINSKI
TECUMSEH, MICHIGAN
18 15

• • • • • • • •

MY SON HAS EXCELLENT EATING HABITS. Ever since he was a kid I got him used to drinking water. I figured if I started him on that it would be a habit in his teenage years. As we speak my son is downstairs working out in our gym. We watched a movie earlier together and he was on my exercise bike as we did. We are both in training because we are going to climb Kilimanjaro together in July.

—FRAN CAPO
FOREST HILLS, NEW YORK
15

• • • • • • • •

I'M THE ONE WHO COOKS for all of my daughter's friends when they come over. I really like having all her friends around. They're not getting in trouble, and I like them all. I'm really lucky.

—B.S.
BROOKLYN, NEW YORK
22 17

• • • • • • • •

MY GIRLS ARE TWO YEARS APART. The top three things they fight over are the car, the phone, and clothes. They generally work things out. My husband and I mediated their shared-car schedule and their home-phone schedule.

—SHARI H.
NOVATO, CALIFORNIA
17 15

IF MY SON WANTS TO GO TO HIS FRIEND'S HOUSE
to play PlayStation but we are going to his
grandma's house that day, he is likely to blow a
fuse. He is old enough to he think he should be
able decide how to spend his time. But if we left
it up to him he'd never visit any of our relatives.
It's a fight we are having more and more frequently.
We just tell him that he has to make time in his
life for all the people who want to see him.

> —*MARGARET BELTON*
> *PARMA, OHIO*
> 13

• • • • • • • •

MY 18-YEAR-OLD ADMIRES HIMSELF IN THE MIRROR
by striking different GQ poses and calling himself
"hot." And while my back is turned or I am not
around, I'm sure they share obscene jokes with
their father because when I hear them all
laughing and ask what's funny, they all say,
"Nothinnnggggg." I miss the Happy Meal and Pull-
Up days, but what an experience it is, having
teenagers. I truly love it!

> —*PAMELA*
> *YONKERS, NEW YORK*

• • • • • • • •

MY HUSBAND AND I HAVE ALWAYS HAD high
expectations for our four kids. They have always
had chores to do, and they are expected to do
them. A few years ago, we went away overnight
to celebrate our anniversary, and my sister-in-law
and niece babysat our kids. I was so proud to
hear that after dinner was over, without even
being asked, my older sons got right up from the
table and helped clear the dishes and put them in
the dishwasher.

> —*JERENE*
> *WILLIAMSPORT, PENNSYLVANIA*
> 13 12 7 7

Kids worry that they're too fat, too thin, or too weak. Have an active household where kids get physical activity every day. This helps teens feel better and worry less about their physical attributes.

—*Erika Karres*
Chapel Hill,
North Carolina
Daughters in
their late 30s

I thought it was important for me to be home when he arrived home from school during junior high. Just because they can unlock the door by themselves doesn't mean they are safe by themselves. I gradually increased the time he could be left alone as he grew up. Now I simply ask him to let me know what his plans are and where he'll be.

—*J.S.*
Houston, Texas
👦 18

• • • • • • • •

I would hang out in the kitchen as long as I could so that when he walked into the house I would be there. It was the best time to connect with him. If I happened to be standing in the kitchen at 11 a.m. Sunday when he woke up, that was prime time. I cut out going to church and the community chorus, which I loved. I stopped going just so I could hang out for those two minutes. It was only for two years, his junior and senior years. Isn't that pathetic? But it worked.

—*Cathy*
Freeport, Maine
👦 19 👧 16

• • • • • • • •

When our oldest son was sixteen, three of his good friends were killed in a car accident; one was his cousin. He was supposed to have gone with them, but he didn't. I think it made my husband a lot closer to the boys. Guys are funny: They don't hug and say, "I love you" all the time. It helped us as a family to just enjoy all of our time together. That's the most important thing about having a teen: Take advantage of every minute.

—*Cathy Westmoreland*
Churchville, Virginia
👧 34 👦 30

WHEN SOMETHING'S NOT RIGHT

My daughter is 5'5" and she used to weigh about 125 pounds. One day, she told us she wanted to lose some weight, so we took her to a doctor, got a weight check, bought her a gym club membership and some running clothes. She started running three times a week.

The compliments started rolling in after she'd dropped a full size. To celebrate, we bought her new clothes. But then, she started dropping even more weight and I got worried. I brought her to the doctor, who told me she was fine and suggested she join the school's cross country team. This cycle continued—her dropping weight, me bringing her to doctors and being told she was fine— until she reached 94 pounds. That was about the time she came to me and admitted she didn't feel well. I sat down and called several doctors right in front of my daughter. It was so frustrating—they ignored us. Finally, in frustration I went with my daughter to a hospital and had them make the call.

What I learned from this is to never give up. If you know deep down that something's wrong, keep pushing one step further until you get the right answers. For two months prior to my daughter getting help, a little voice inside of me had been saying something wasn't right. I only wish I would've acted on it sooner.

—*P.O.*
NEW BRUNSWICK, NEW JERSEY
18 15

The boys are very different from each other. They fight over everything, even the color of the sky. But they also look out for, and are protective of, each other.

—MARILYN BANKS
  PACIFICA,
  CALIFORNIA
  21 16

I ONCE MET A MOTHER OF FIVE KIDS. When I asked her what she did for a living, she said she used to be an attorney. When I asked her what she did now, she said she stays home. I expressed surprise because her kids were in their teens, but she explained that it's more important to be home when your kids are teens than when they're younger.

—SUSIE WALTON
  SAN DIEGO, CALIFORNIA
  28 26 24 22

IF YOU CAN REALLY STAY IN THE MOMENT with your teenager, that's when the best things happen. One time, I spilled grape soda on the counter and I was trying to get it out. I had one of those Mr. Clean Magic Erasers and I said, "What else can we clean?" Robert kept saying "Oh, my God, you could be a commercial for these things." We just started laughing. Moments like that are just so real.

—MARY ANN GABRIEL
  FRANKLIN, MASSACHUSETTS
  16 12

BOTH OF MY KIDS SWEAR like truck drivers. I tell them if they want to talk like that they better join the Navy. They're too old for me to wash their mouths out with soap now. Not that I did it when they were young, either: Maybe that's the problem.

—L.B.
  BRADDOCK, PENNSYLVANIA
  16 14

JUST LET THEM KEEP THEIR ROOM in any condition they want. It's not going to help anyone for you to keep screaming about them not picking up stuff in there. It's their room and they should be able to do what they want with it and live in it however they see fit. In the rest of the house it's a different story. You can't let them be a slob in the living room or the kitchen. Those are your rooms.

—*BETTY SMITH*
PITTSBURGH, PENNSYLVANIA
41 28

ASSIGN CHORES TO DO. One of my daughters is responsible for emptying out the two cat litter boxes, while the other daughter feeds the cats and changes their water. Along the same lines, one daughter empties the dishwasher, while the other daughter fills it. My teenage daughter sometimes does laundry, as well. They don't get allowances for these jobs; they're just expected to do them as members of the family.

—*ANNMARIE PEARSON*
GIG HARBOR, WASHINGTON
15 10 6

Fun things to do with teens are camping and going to the movies.

—*BONNIE LAMB*
CHICAGO, ILLINOIS
23 20

ALLOW FOR HEALTHY REBELLION at the age-appropriate time. My kids don't hang up their clothes in their rooms, but I don't choose that as a battle. I only choose those that have to do with health, safety and welfare. I get excited if the room is a fire hazard, like if there are so many posters on the wall. But a messy room with clothes on the floor is a way for them to rebel. It's better to let them rebel at home than for them to go off to college and do it then.

—*JOBETH MCLEOD*
SAN ANTONIO, TEXAS
26 18

QUALITY TIME

When my kids were in high school, our lives were so hectic that, being the organized workaholic I am, I decided I would schedule two hours every Wednesday to spend with one of them. They'd rotate weekly, so, once a month, I was guaranteed some quality time with each one.

My plan started off badly when I tried to force my oldest son to spend our bonding time helping me finish household chores. For two hours, I ordered him to hand me light bulbs or screw drivers, and he did. Needless to say, it wasn't a very communicative time. My kids teased me for this, until I finally figured out that instead of trying to multitask during our bonding time, I should actually pay attention to them.

From that point on, things got much better. We'd either sit in their rooms and talk, or go to a park, or listen to music. Sometimes those two hours turned into a lot more, but we always stuck with it. I think that when you have a very busy family, it's far too easy to let relationships fall by the wayside if you don't have something concrete planned. Those two hours a week were one of the best investments I've ever made because they soothed my guilt feelings as parent and allowed me to keep in touch with my kids.

—MICHAEL
SOUTH BELOIT, ILLINOIS
34 32 30 26

TEACH YOUR TEENAGER HOW TO DO CHORES like cooking, laundry and cleaning. My ex-husband always got on me for teaching my son how to do laundry, but when he went into the service, he had to know that.

—*N. GRELL*
PIPE CREEK, TEXAS
38 36 34 32

WHEN SIBLINGS FIGHT, they suddenly become very eager to spill each other's secrets to you as a means of getting revenge. To get the best, most detailed information possible out of them, use reverse psychology. When one of your kids comes up and says, "I know something really bad about so-and-so," the perfect response is to fake a disinterested look and say, "I don't want you to tell me anything that your brother or sister said in confidence." For whatever reason, this suddenly makes them *really* eager to talk. This is when you learn a lot.

—*ANTHONY MANUEL*
KINDER, LOUISIANA
17 14 11

MY DAUGHTER IS NOT ALLOWED to make or receive phone calls after 10 p.m., and the length of her phone calls cannot exceed 20 minutes. I was raised with this rule and it just seems to make sense to me now. She has tried to sneak phone calls after 10, but I've always caught her and she has lost phone privileges for the next two nights. This seems to put a damper on her nightly phone calling. And it makes other parents happy that their phone is not ringing at all hours of the night.

—*TRACIE DESHIELDS*
CHANDLER, INDIANA
14 11

WHEN MY SONS WERE TEENS, I made extra sure to be at home. For one thing, when they wanted to talk to me I was there! But also, it took a lot of pressure off of them: If their friends were looking for a place to hang out without parents around, they wouldn't be interested coming to our house because I was there. In fact, they were always *encouraged* to come to our house. Many a night, I cooked spaghetti dinner for 15 hungry teens!

—*SUSIE WALTON*
SAN DIEGO, CALIFORNIA
😊 28 😊 26 😊 24 😊 22

• • • • • • • •

WHEN MY DAUGHTER WAS ABOUT 15 she went through a period when she was on the phone just about every minute she was home. It was like the phone was glued to the side of her head. We threatened, we punished, but every time we turned around she was still on the phone. So we made her pay the phone bill. When she thought we were kidding we didn't pay the bill and the phone company shut the service off. We knew the phone was important enough to her that she'd come around. After she paid the bill for a couple months and realized what kind of charges she was running up she started talking on the phone a lot less often.

—*HOWARD OLLEN*
STRUTHERS, OHIO
👧 20

• • • • • • • •

I just hung around the house. Even if she didn't speak to me, I provided a focus for her anger.

—*N.*
BROOKLYN, NEW YORK
👧 17

PULL A RABBIT OUT OF THE HAT

For my 16th birthday, I begged my parents for a car. They always said no, because it was too expensive. The big day came, and I received a very nice, brand-new stereo system and lots of clothes, but no car. Two weeks later, my family was debating what to do for dinner when my mom announced, "Get dressed! We're going to McDonalds!" I thought this was weird— for us, "going out to dinner" usually meant a sit-down-and-order place, like Chili's. Even stranger was the fact that my mom insisted on bringing a camera. "We haven't sent the grandparents any good pictures of you kids for awhile," she explained.

At McDonalds, we ate, snapped some photos, then headed back out to the parking lot. That's when I noticed someone had parked my dream car—a red convertible Rabbit—right next to my mom's minivan. "Oh, my God! Look at that!" I shrieked, pointing. My dad, who usually got angry when I brought up cars, simply smiled. Much to my surprise, he walked right up to it and started inspecting the body. "Too bad it's not for sale," he said casually, reaching for the driver's side door and cracking it open. "Jeff! Shut that! You can't go around opening other people's doors!" My mom responded, scowling. "Relax, Cheri, I was only checking the mileage," he replied, obeying her nonetheless. I couldn't believe my good luck; was my dad taking happy pills or something? "I'd love to test drive these sometime!" I blurted out. In response, my father looked me straight in the eye and replied, "How about right now?" He then reached into his pocket and pulled out the keys.

This happened ten years ago, but I still remember the moment as though it were yesterday. If you want to be a cool parent, look for a way to catch your teenager off guard when giving big gifts. The extra effort my parents put into giving me my car illustrated more clearly than any words could have just how far they were willing to go for their children.

—*Shannon Hurd*
Castle Rock, Colorado

I REMEMBER THAT WHEN I WAS A TEENAGER I liked to sleep in on the weekends. I could easily sleep until noon or later every day if my dad didn't come in to get me out of bed. Now I'm not so sure they should have let me do that. I think it would be good for parents to get their teenagers in work mode while they are still in school so that the transition from the high school years to the working years isn't so tough. Don't be afraid to roust those kids out of bed. You can find something for them to do around the house.

—*DAN SANTOS*
GREENTREE, PENNSYLVANIA
20

"I've been working with teenagers for 28 years now and I've learned that the basic kid is still the basic kid. If they have a good family life, they'll usually be fine."

—*FRANK MOTTA, HIGH SCHOOL PRINCIPAL*
PALM DESERT, CALIFORNIA

ALL YOUR KIDS WANT IS YOUR TIME. When I was a teenager, my dad and I played a lot of golf and basketball together. Once a month, we'd take off a Monday. Against my mother's better judgment, I'd skip school to play golf or go fishing with him.

—*STEVEN SHELTON*
WICHITA FALLS, TEXAS
30 22

I MADE A POINT OF HAVING DINNER with my teenage daughters every night, and we played board games together. I remember the laughter in our house so well that it still touches me!

—*VIRGINIA T.*
CHICAGO, ILLINOIS
34 34 29 26

• • • • • • • •

I TRIED TO SPEND AS MUCH TIME with my teenagers as I could. My oldest girl was an early riser like me, so we often went out for breakfast together and then shopping or to the art museum downtown. These were special times because I knew she would be more involved with her friends and off to college in just a few short years.

—*JOHN R. BRIGHT*
ALLENTOWN, PENNSYLVANIA
33 31

• • • • • • • •

JOIN A READING CIRCLE WITH YOUR KIDS. I know it might sound boring but it can be a great experience. My daughter and I joined one a year ago and we love it. She will talk to me about the books we are reading during dinner, or when she gets home from school. It's a real bonding experience and lots of fun.

—*MARY WEBB*
WHEELING, WEST VIRGINIA
15 13

• • • • • • • •

WE LIKE GOING TO THE MOVIES TOGETHER. We especially like going to opening nights. We also like going to hockey games at a big arena. When we can get together, it's a blast.

—*JERRY*
EAST NORTHPORT, NEW YORK
16 2

My son only gets privacy when he's home. When he's out, I snoop.

—*DENISE L.*
CHICAGO, ILLINOIS
13

VACATIONS WITH TEENS (NO, REALLY!)

ON VACATIONS, DO THINGS THAT INTEREST THEM. One year, while at Cape Cod, where my kids insist there is nothing to do, we let them both go to a drag show in Provincetown. They had a blast and talked about it for days, particularly because it was risqué and that they were allowed to see a more adult venue. They have done other things there, too, such as take in a windsurfing lesson, go horseback riding and bike, but it was fun to let them take in an evening, safe, adult excursion.

—ANN HAALAND
HIGHLAND, NEW YORK
🐾 23 🐾 20

• • • • • • • • •

HAVE A WHINE-FREE VACATION: It's possible! One year, I told my kids, who were then 13 and 11, that at the end of each day of vacation I would give them each $5. Their eyes grew big as platters, thinking of what they could buy. But then I told them that every time they whined, I would deduct $1. It worked like a charm! Most days both kids earned $5, and a few days $4. One day my son whined because he was only getting $4, so he got $3. That was the first and only time that happened! Besides having a nearly whine-free vacation, I think this technique taught my teens consequences, responsibility, and how to save and spend money.

—JEAN NICK
KINTNERSVILLE, PENNSYLVANIA
🐾 16 🐾 14

• • • • • • • • •

GET THEM THEIR OWN ROOM AT THE HOTEL. I wasn't about to sit around for hours on my vacation waiting for my daughter to get out of the bathroom. Leave them in the room and let them order room service and watch TV. And when you hear gripes about an activity you've planned, say, "Humor me."

—PAT CURRY
ATHENS, GEORGIA
🐾 17 🐾 15

A GREAT EXPERIENCE FOR YOUR TEEN IS A MISSION TRIP to a third-world country. My older daughter wanted to go to Haiti with her dad. We challenged her to raise at least $100 of the $1,000. She raised all of it.

> —*ANONYMOUS*
> *ATLANTA, GEORGIA*
> 16 14

WE'D BE GOING THROUGH THE MOST GORGEOUS SCENERY on a summer vacation in Colorado and my kids would be in the backseat with their noses in books. It made me so mad. Kids don't always share all your interests, but when we'd get to the top of that mountain and throw snowballs at each other, I knew the trip was worth it.

> —*M.F.*
> *BUFFALO GROVE, ILLINOIS*
> 21 20

EACH SUMMER, IT WAS VERY IMPORTANT TO ME that we travel together someplace as a family. Some years it was to the mountains and other years we visited family in Maui. But the key was to do something together. I think it helped to keep us all close.

> —*SUSIE WALTON*
> *SAN DIEGO, CALIFORNIA*
> 28 26 24 22

GO ON VACATIONS WITH ANOTHER FAMILY with kids the same age as your own. For one week during the summer, we go to a cabin on a private island together, and it's great. The kids look forward to being with someone their own age, so they're excited and better behaved. The adults are happy to have people to talk to as well, so they're less likely to snap at the kids if things do get crazy.

> —*KATHY MCCLINTIC*
> *CENTENNIAL, COLORADO*
> 27 23

HOW MANY FOOD GROUPS?

More than 70 percent of teens don't eat an adequate number of vegetable servings per day, and roughly half of all teens skimp on fruits and dairy products.

MY DAUGHTER HAS GOTTEN INTO ROCK CLIMBING. One night at about nine thirty, freezing cold outside, she said she wanted to go rock climbing. She called up a friend and asked me, "Dad, can you take us rock climbing?" My first thought was to say no. But I said yes; and we ended up having a good time.

—BOB G.
VIRGINIA BEACH, VIRGINIA
👶21 👧16

• • • • • • • •

PLAN FAMILY GAME NIGHTS, but not on a Saturday night or some night when they'd be mortified to stay home with the family. Our kids moan about it, but mostly just for show. Secretly, I think they look forward to it. Certainly, once we get going, they really enjoy it. We're competitive, silly, and, for once, not focused on work, school, or family issues.

—K. JONES
PHILADELPHIA PENNSYLVANIA
👧14 👶10 👶6

• • • • • • • •

OUR FAMILY WALKS OUR TWO DOGS every evening after dinner, without fail. This is a great time to talk about concerns in the dark so that if eye contact is difficult it can be avoided. We also try very hard to keep the lines of communication open so that our child feels free to talk to us. Even if she knows we may be angry, she knows we're on her side. For example, my child was open with us that she'd been dropped from the "challenge" English program for indifferent grades last year. She could have kept quiet about this and we may not have found out until well into the term, if at all.

—BRENDA KILGORE
PHOENIX, CANBERRA, AUSTRALIAN CAPITAL TERRITORY, AUSTRALIA
👧15

BAKE WITH YOUR TEENAGERS. It works well with young teenage girls. It's like an arts-and-crafts project, but since they get to use real kitchen equipment and come up with a real dessert, it also makes them feel very grown up. I only loosely supervise, so that they don't feel like I'm hovering. But I don't think they mind when I pop in occasionally and taste the batter.

—*J.D.*
BALTIMORE, MARYLAND
🐵 *15* 🐵 *3*

• • • • • • • • •

FIND AN INTEREST THAT YOU HAVE IN COMMON and do it together. With my son, that's our little dog. He loves to play with our pooch and teach her new tricks. I'll think of a new trick to teach her, or suggest taking her for a walk. He never says no to that. However, he declines, or at least doesn't jump for joy, over other activities. Go to lunch with Mom? Forget it. Go to a movie with Mom? No, thanks.

—*ANONYMOUS*
LITTLETON, COLORADO
🐵 *19* 🐵 *13*

• • • • • • • • •

SET UP GROUND RULES about when your kids' friends come over and where they go in your house. Once, around the time my daughter was starting to date, I took a shower during the day. And when I walked out of the bathroom, I was suddenly greeted by my daughter's new friend. I saw him down the hall and I sprung like a jackrabbit back into the bathroom. I talked to my daughter that day. I said, "Next time you have people over, warn me. Check with what I'm doing!"

—*DIANE BLOVET*
KENNESAW, GEORGIA
🐵 *39* 🐵 *36* 🐵 *26*

We rarely get to eat dinner at the same time, so our family time is watching old movies after homework and chores are done, just before bedtime.

—*N.*
BROOKLYN, NEW YORK
🐵 *17*

MOST IMPORTANT ROOM IN THE HOUSE

WE SET UP A KITCHEN TIMER OUTSIDE THE BATHROOM. The girls can stay in as long as they want, if nobody else wants to use it. But if somebody does and the bathroom's occupied, she starts the timer for three minutes and gives a warning. It cuts down on shouting.

> —*SEAN H.*
> *NEW YORK, NEW YORK*
> 👧 *14* 👧 *12*

• • • • • • • •

WE GOT EACH OF THE OLDER GIRLS little cabinets to keep in their rooms, along with big mirrors and good lighting. They can do a lot of their primping there, and save the bathroom for things that require running water!

> —*LUZ*
> *SAN DIEGO, CALIFORNIA*
> 👧 *14* 👧 *12* 👧 *5*

• • • • • • • •

MY 18-YEAR-OLD SON AND 16-YEAR-OLD DAUGHTER share a bathroom. For the last few years we have the same argument every morning: Who gets the bathroom first? We have tried schedules, timers—nothing seemed to work. Recently, I decided that my daughter should have the bathroom first with a time limit. At first she would take longer and my son would be banging on the door, desperate to use the facilities. Then one morning I didn't hear any yelling or banging on the bathroom door. I thought, "Finally, they worked it out." After about a week of these quiet mornings, I complimented my children. They both gave me with the strangest look. My daughter admitted that she still was running overtime in the bathroom. When I asked my son why he wasn't complaining, he rolled his eyes. Then he said, "Well, Mom, you said work it out and I decided I would just go outside to pee." Thank goodness we live in the country!

> —*J.B.C.*
> *BROOKSVILLE, FLORIDA*
> 👦 *18* 👧 *16*

MY STEPDAUGHTERS LOVE TO SHOP. It's a good way to bond with teenage girls. I try something on and they get excited and say, "Oh! You have to buy this!"

> —*ELISE COLLINS*
> *SAN FRANCISCO, CALIFORNIA*
> 🧒 *18* 🧒 *15* 🧒 *5*

• • • • • • • •

IF YOU GET INTO A YELLING MATCH with your teen, yell "B.I.O.N.I.C." I got that from an ex-Marine who is now a motivational speaker. I did that with my daughter. It made her stop to think, "What's B.I.O.N.I.C?" It means: Believe it or not, I care. If you explain it when you are calm, then when you get into that heated moment, you yell this and it defuses the situation.

> —*THOMAS M.W. "MIKE" DOWNS*
> *FAYETTEVILLE, NEW YORK*
> 🧒 *20* 🧒 *16* 🧒 *13* 🧒 *10*

• • • • • • • •

I FEEL VERY OLD. He's getting bigger and stronger than me, and his shoe size is bigger than mine. The flip side is, you can have what I call the golden nuggets with them; when you do have some time with them and you do something fun and talk with them. They are real people now. They have real thoughts and desires, and if you can get them to share them with you, it can be very special. We did a bike ride across Georgia when he turned 13. It was 428 miles. We spent a whole week together, and leading up to it we spent every weekend riding together getting ready for it. Saturday and Sunday: 60-, 70-, 80-mile rides. I wouldn't trade that for the world. You have to go out of your way to find the golden nuggets. I wasn't interested in riding a bike, but he loved it so I did it with him.

> —*DANIEL*
> *ATLANTA, GEORGIA*
> 🧒 *14* 🧒 *12* 🧒 *5*

Make sure they get their sleep. Sometimes it seems all teens do is eat and sleep. Teens who get the sleep they need have better grades and better moods. Because of this, I make sure that my eighth grader has strict bedtime rules.

—*JEAN NICK*
KINTNERSVILLE,
PENNSYLVANIA
16 14

TAKE AN INTEREST IN WHAT YOUR TEEN is into. My daughter loves Orlando Bloom. She buys the teen magazines and has his posters all over her walls. I try to be interested in those things. I'll ask her about articles she's read about him. The benefit is that I know what she's interested in, and she knows I'm interested in what she is interested in. I could really care less about Orlando Bloom, but if I were to brush it off, I'd miss an opportunity to talk with her. I don't remember my mom doing that.

—*CHERYL NORTON*
WASHOUGAL, WASHINGTON
13

• • • • • • • •

ONCE, MY HUSBAND AND I WENT to Disney World with our youngest daughter. We were going to stay the night and my son and daughter—ages 17 and 15—were going to be at home on their own. They knew they weren't allowed to have anybody over. After spending time at Disney World, my husband said, "You know what, let's just go home and we'll call on the way." When we were close to home we called and said we were coming home. When we got home, everything looked fine. A few days later I started finding six-pack rings in strange places: I found one around the chandelier. Then they confessed. They didn't expect us home and cleaned up real quick when they heard we were coming. We sat them down and told them, "If we trust you enough to leave you at home, please do as we say." And we still trusted them after that. They were good kids.

—*DIANE BLOVET*
KENNNESAW, GEORGIA
39 36 26

The Six-Year Stretch: Achieving (or Not) in School

Do well but have fun. Study hard but don't forget about the football game. Play sports but get ready for college. The mixed messages of the teen years often collide with a crash (and a crush?) at school. The trick is to help your teen find a balance—or, in some cases, just get to homeroom on time.

SCHOOL SEEMS TO BE ONE OF THOSE THINGS she knows she has to complete in order to do what she wants in life. There are good days where she is eager to go and a few days where it takes a major fight to get her out of the door.

—*RITA PORTER*
SPRINGFIELD, MISSOURI
14

IF ALL ELSE FAILS, THERE'S ALWAYS BOARDING SCHOOL.

—*JAY KLEBANOFF*
NORFOLK, VIRGINIA

THEY SAY YOU HAVE TO PICK YOUR BATTLES with kids, and I think insisting they do well in school at practically any cost is one of those battles worth fighting. You have to insist on excellence: You have to make your kids understand that their entire future hinges on excelling in school. Take no excuses. There's too much at stake to let them goof off through high school.

—*BRITTANY MELLOR*
ZELIENOPLE, PENNSYLVANIA
🐾 *14*

• • • • • • • •

ALL THROUGH MIDDLE SCHOOL, my daughter had straight A's. Education is very important in our family, and we frequently talk about how important it is to do well in school. I think my daughter interpreted these speeches to mean we expected her to get perfect grades every semester. As soon as she started high school, I noticed she was getting really stressed out. I took her aside and made it very clear that getting straight A's wasn't our expectation; doing her best was. She calmed down visibly once she heard this, which taught me that sometimes it's important to state what seems obvious.

—*ANONYMOUS*
CLEVELAND, OHIO
🐾 *14* 🐾 *11*

• • • • • • • •

MY DAUGHTER HAD A PROBLEM RELATING to a teacher in school. I took a proactive approach and met with them separately and resolved the matter without any damage. You need to be that involved and head off problems before they become massive.

—*S.S.*
PASSAIC, NEW JERSEY
FOUR KIDS AGES 23-40

ORGANIZATION IS A HUGE ISSUE for 13-year-olds, so teach them to use a planner. They put off school projects until the last minute, and they never bring copies of their game schedules with them. Of course, then they will call, saying, "You need to pick me up now!"

—*HEIDI BROWN*
PIPE CREEK, TEXAS
13 7 4

• • • • • • • • •

I SEPARATED MY OLDEST BOYS IN SCHOOL because of competition. My oldest is a star: A real over-achiever, studied a lot, played high school baseball. My middle is very bright, but not as motivated academically, and was always looking to get attention, cheating on exams, skipping class. He was better off in private school where he didn't have to walk through the school corridors being reminded by teachers and school administrators that he looks just like his brother. We found outlets other than sports for him. He's a phenomenal photographer and still really enjoys that.

—*ANONYMOUS*
SAN FRANCISCO, CALIFORNIA
27 24 18

• • • • • • • • •

MY 16-YEAR-OLD SON IS GOING THROUGH a phase right now and I had to go talk to his principal. I told my son, "As long as you go to school and you're on time for class, you're going to pick up on things around you and you're going to get good grades. If you get bad grades you're going to go to summer school or night school, which is the last thing you want to do."

—*ARMAND MONTIEL*
SAN DIEGO, CALIFORNIA
16

I see teenage life as a stool with three legs. The legs are the parent, the school, and the student. If the stool is missing one leg, then it can't stand.

—*KAREN*
KNOXVILLE,
TENNESSEE
17 14

MY FLAG-BURNING TEEN

My advice on raising teenagers is: *Just get them through it!* When my son started junior high school, trouble just seemed to follow him. I became quite friendly with the vice-principal—we were on a first-name basis. I knew we had really become close when the vice-principal called me one day and the first words out of his mouth were, "I have your son in my office, and frankly, I think he needs professional counseling." It seems that my son was in gym class waiting with the other boys for class to start. They were talking about the student assembly earlier that day where all students received a small replica of the American Flag. Well, someone handed my son a lighter and dared him to light the flag, and of course, he did—just when the coach walked out of his office. To try and hide his actions, my flag-burning son dropped the flag under the bleachers, and set the bleachers on fire. Thus, another trip to the office and another call to me from my friend, the vice-principal.

This is just one of many instances of the fun times the teenage years provided our family. Just get them through it—believe it or not, you will be able to look back and laugh about it one of these days. My son, who I was quite positive would turn out to be a convict, is now a 28-year-old architect, married to a wonderful young lady, and they are both upstanding members of their community.

—*P. LEONARD*
GREENWOOD, ARIZONA
28 25

CHECK THEIR HOMEWORK AND TESTS, long before the report card comes. One son who normally got great grades in math came home with a D on his report card. We hadn't noticed the deterioration in his grades because we'd been too complacent. We stayed on top of his grades, and our daughter's, after that, even when we thought they were doing well.

—*JEN W.*
SAN CARLOS, CALIFORNIA
24 22 19

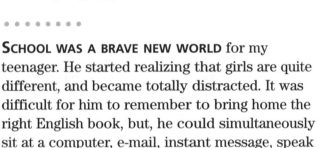

SCHOOL WAS A BRAVE NEW WORLD for my teenager. He started realizing that girls are quite different, and became totally distracted. It was difficult for him to remember to bring home the right English book, but, he could simultaneously sit at a computer, e-mail, instant message, speak on the cell phone, and entertain whoever was at our house.

—*BOB FITZSIMMONS*

DON'T LET OTHER PARENTS make you feel guilty about your decisions. I can't tell you how many times my husband and I have been lectured by other parents who believe we should've made our sons take out student loans and pay their own tuition. My husband and I felt that putting our sons through college was something we could give them in life that they'd always have. As for the argument that paying their own way would teach them responsibility? Please: They already had plenty of responsibilities—to their classes, to their friends, and to their teammates.

—*JANIS HACKETT*
CENTENNIAL, COLORADO
36 32 26 24

TEEN TOPIC

Only twenty-five percent of teenagers know that the U.S. Constitution was written in Philadelphia, but 75 percent of teenagers know that the zip code 90210 is for Beverly Hills, California.

WE TRY TO HELP OUR DAUGHTER handle pressure by setting realistic goals and expectations. We do not expect top grades all the time, for example. We are happy if teachers' comments indicate she is working. We try to focus on what our child does very well, such as violin and drums, and the wonderful network of friends she has established, rather than giving the impression she has to be perfect at everything.

—*Brenda Kilgore*
Phoenix, Canberra, Australian Capital Territory, Australia
🐷 15

• • • • • • • •

IT'S A CONSTANT TUG-OF-WAR with my daughter about lateness and homework. She has the potential to get into a very good college if she applies herself, but this semester she's been late for school eight times. And she frequently procrastinates on doing her homework until the night before it is due. It causes me pain to watch this happen, but I finally came to the conclusion that I can't keep bailing her out: I have to let her make her own mistakes. This is a huge realization for me—someone who has always defined herself by her role as a mom. The fact is, whatever kind of person she's going to be is pretty much set by now.

—*M.C.*
Denver, Colorado
🐷 16 😊 13

• • • • • • • •

THE RULE IN OUR HOUSE IS that homework may not be done with television or music being played. To ensure this, my husband and I moved a desk into our study and we insist that this is where Matt does his homework when he begins high school this year. He's not thrilled, but too bad.

—*Mary Medland*
Baltimore, Maryland
😊 14

IT'S NOW OR LATER: HOMEWORK

KIDS NEED A BREAK AFTER SCHOOL. Instead of making my kids do their homework right when they get home, I give them time to get a snack and run around outside. This gives them a chance to unwind. It gets dark so early during the school year that otherwise they wouldn't have the chance to play outside.

> —*DEB UHLER*
> *HELLERTOWN, PENNSYLVANIA*
> 14 10

WE HAVE A RULE IN OUR HOUSE: Homework first, then play. When I was a kid, my parents didn't make me do my homework when I got home from school. So I'd procrastinate, and then late at night I'd be stressed, frantically trying to get it done before bedtime. When our kids get home from school, they're allowed to get a snack, and then they do their homework. This way, they get it out of the way and we can all enjoy our dinner and family time afterwards.

> —*ANNMARIE PEARSON*
> *GIG HARBOR, WASHINGTON*
> 15 10 6

WE HAVE A STRICT RULE: No television before homework—ever! This rule actually started when the kids were in first grade and continues now. They complain, but they know the rule.

> —*J.S.H.*
> *HOUSTON, TEXAS*
> 16 14 10

MY SON'S SENIOR YEAR IN HIGH SCHOOL was hard for all of us because he was never a very good student, he never quite fit the structured mode of academia and he was diagnosed with ADD. By his senior year he was goofing off and cutting classes. We didn't know until the day of gradua-tion whether he'd be able to participate. The only things that seemed to help were channeling his energies into something constructive that he liked doing. He loved going to summer camp and would come home happy and feeling really good about himself. When he was 16, he got interested in the Civil War and immersed himself in learning about it. We outfitted him and encouraged him to join a Civil War reenactment group. After he graduated, we sent him off to Germany for the summer and that was a good learning experience for him—he ended up staying a full year.

> —*ELAINE*
> *SEATTLE, WASHINGTON*
> 😊 *24* 👧 *17*

• • • • • • • •

WE EXPERIENCED A DRAMATIC DIFFERENCE in my daughter's school performance starting in the eighth grade, and it wasn't until twelfth grade that she showed a consistent interest in working well in school. But we had a terrible time with her. We tried everything to keep her in school: We grounded her, took away her allowance, talked with her calmly, spent quality time with her, talked with her peers, sent her to counseling, and even let her take a correspondence course for a year. Ultimately, we found that you have to keep trying different things and keep letting the child know you love them.

> —*MARIAH*
> *TORONTO, ONTARIO, CANADA*
> 😊 *24* 😊 *23* 👧 *18*

IF SHE DOES SOMETHING WRONG, I don't come unglued. One time, she brought home a progress report with a D. She'd never gotten anything less than an A. She was worried about how we'd react, but we didn't crush her spirit. We advised her on how to fix it. By the end of the semester, it was fixed.

—*CHIP NORTON*
WASHOUGAL, WASHINGTON
13

· · · · · · · ·

" I'm convinced I was in school more than my son for a few years. I went to so many parent-teacher meetings about my son's tendency to hang out in the park instead of his classes that I should have gotten the diploma! "

—*ANONYMOUS*
CHARLESTON, SOUTH CAROLINA
18 15 12 2

· · · · · · · ·

PARENTS NEED TO SHOW HOW AND WHY school-work is relevant to the child's life and future aspirations, and to make sure school has meaning and worth to the child.

—*BEV WALTON-PORTER*
COLORADO SPRINGS, COLORADO
14

DROPPING OUT

My oldest son—I call him my late bloomer—was always a happy kid, and he was very headstrong. Once he made up his mind about something, it was tough to change his opinion. His stubbornness did not make his teenage years easy for my wife and me to deal with. He made excellent grades in school up to the tenth grade, when his group of friends changed and his studies started to suffer. I don't know how many times I went to school to talk to the teachers. He got to a point where he was failing school, and at the start of his senior year he dropped out. Needless to say, my wife and I were devastated. We wondered what to do, we questioned where we had gone wrong, and we did not understand why this was happening. We decided the only approach was one of unconditional love and support. My son worked a couple of odd jobs through the following summer. We assured him we would not give up on him and would stand behind him. Most important, we assured him that we still loved him. Eventually, he earned his GED, which was a tremendous boost for his confidence and outlook on life. He went to work as a jailer for the city, worked there for seven years went to the Sheriff's office for four years, and now works for the Department of Homeland Security. He also joined the Air Force Reserve and has been in for 12 years now. He is 33 years old and happily married, with three great kids. I lost my hair with this one; but it was worth it, he's a great guy.

—ANONYMOUS
OKLAHOMA CITY, OKLAHOMA

WHEN MY SON WAS IN THE ELEVENTH GRADE, my husband and I were told that he was mouthing off to his teachers. My husband decided to sit in on the classes and see exactly what the problem was. When we told my son that his dad was going to do that, you could have heard my son's scream—"Noooooooooo!"—all over town. And that was the end of that; we never had another problem with him in that regard.

—*ANONYMOUS*
  DES MOINES, IOWA

. . . .

IF PARENTS CAN AFFORD IT, kids shouldn't hold part-time jobs. There are too many other things that come up, like study groups, dances and sporting events. Part of the joy of being young is getting to experience these things firsthand. None of my children has ever worked during the school year. If they want to earn extra money, I assign them chores around the house, which also benefits our family.

—*LENNARD HAYNES SR.*
  HOUSTON, TEXAS
  17 16 15 14 12

. . . .

IF YOU HAVEN'T ESTABLISHED the importance of studying by the time your kids are teenagers, it is too late. Studying is something you have to get them in the habit of doing very early in their education. If kids get to be 12 or 13 and still have bad study habits it will be very hard to change them. At that point you have to be very hands-on and work with them individually as much as your schedule allows.

—*BECKY LAKE*
  BADEN, PENNSYLVANIA
  21 16 13

One way to have a good relationship with your child is to send him or her to boarding school! I believe that my daughter is going to get a whole lot out of college, because she's already dealt with many of the issues kids face when they leave home.

—*ANONYMOUS*
  WAKEFIELD,
  NEW HAMPSHIRE
  26 17

THEY WERE ON THEIR OWN when it came to their homework. I didn't feel it was my place to be a tutor. They had their job, which was to go to class, understand what they were learning (and if not, tell the teacher what their problem was), come home, and do their homework on their own. If I asked if they did their homework and they said, "yes," I took it that they did. If they said, "not yet," I'd remind them it was their job to do it and to get it done or they would suffer the consequences the next day in class.

—*SUE LYNN*
FORT LAUDERDALE, FLORIDA
👩 *50* 👩 *46* 👩 *45*

• • • • • • • •

WE HAD A TRADITION: Whenever one of my girls was preparing for prom or homecoming, we'd leave the other kids at home with Dad, go out to dinner, and then shop until we found the perfect dress and shoes. It's important to create special one-on-one bonding time with each child.

—*CHERI HURD*
LITTLETON, COLORADO
👩 *26* 👦 *23* 👩 *21* 👦 *14*

• • • • • • • •

EXTRACURRICULAR ACTIVITIES GIVE THEM incredible self-esteem. The problem with teens is socialization. In the suburbs, we hide in our house and watch TV. You have to push your kids to get together with other kids. The extracurricular activities at school have replaced the casual socialization of just going out and playing ball.

—*D.B.*
ATLANTA, GEORGIA
👦 *14* 👦 *12* 👦 *5*

A PROM NIGHT TO REMEMBER

WHEN MY DAUGHTER INFORMED ME that she wanted to spend the night of her senior prom in a hotel with her boyfriend, I said, "Fine, I'll make the reservation. Your boyfriend is welcome to stay in our room." She wasn't too happy about this, but I tried to make it fun. I ordered pizza, provided soda, and stayed in the room all night with her, her boyfriend, her boyfriend's brother and his friend. I did it because I wanted to avoid putting my daughter into a situation where she might be pressured into having sex. If I were there, then she wouldn't have to take the heat for her decision. I firmly believe it's a parent's job to limit the opportunities your kids have for making wrong decisions.

> —*DEBBIE REDDEN-BRUNELLO*
> *TEMECULA, CALIFORNIA*
> 18 16

· · · · · · · · ·

MY STEPDAUGHTER AND I BOUGHT HER PROM DRESS 1,000 miles away from home. She wanted a unique dress, different from the gowns her friends were buying at the mall, so while in Dallas, Texas, two months before prom, we went dress hunting. After five hours and two stores, she chose a black satin, strapless, bell-shaped dress. It was gorgeous! Everyone in the shop commented on the way it fit her hourglass figure. I guess the $200 was worth it, because she won the prize for best dress.

> —*ANONYMOUS*
> *CHICAGO, ILLINOIS*
> 24 20 19 17 15

MY 17-YEAR-OLD SON KNOWS that guitars are chick magnets. He is an excellent musician. He played sax for three years but he got bored with it. He picked up guitar and basically taught himself the first year, and he took it to camp the first year. Hey man, it's changed his whole outlook. It's given him a lot of self-confidence.

—RICHARD GLUCK
ATLANTA, GEORGIA
17 16 12

⁶⁶ For my kids, sports are a way to make sure they keep their grades up. My rule is, your grades have to remain the same or better when you're playing the sport. Education comes first. ⁹⁹

—KAREN
KNOXVILLE, TENNESSEE
17 14

GETTING KIDS TO GO TO SCHOOL can be tough—they don't want to go! My husband and I just explain to our kids that going to school is their job. It's as simple as that. We tell them that they have to go to school so that they can be prepared for work and become productive people in society. It's non-negotiable.

—ANNMARIE PEARSON
GIG HARBOR, WASHINGTON
15 10 6

BY THE TIME A CHILD IS IN HIGH SCHOOL it is no longer the parents' responsibility to intervene in homework and school situations. If a child can't find his own motivation and interest by then, he'll never make it through college. However, I think we can act as advisors, encouraging our children to find their proper niche in school and helping them with the school bureaucracy. When my daughter was in high school, she was always complaining about adults' biased attitude towards teens, especially in light of the Columbine shooting, which had just occurred. I encouraged her to take a class in journalism, where she could spread her opinions to more listeners than just her mother. Somewhat to my surprise, she followed my advice and by her senior year was editor of the opinion section. It was a good thing for her; she needed this sort of outlet.

> —G.B.
> LOS ANGELES, CALIFORNIA
> 🐾 21 😊 14

• • • • • • • •

THE BIGGEST CHALLENGE WE HAD involving sports was when their team's basketball coach became a rage-a-holic. This wasn't just a little yelling; the coach treated the kids with enormous disrespect. The parents tried to have the coach removed, but to no avail. It was so bad that most of the team left or moved to other sports. My sons decided to transfer to the Catholic school in town where they had a wonderful coach. But generally, sports are incredibly positive for teens, keeping them busy, teaching them how to follow directions, and showing them how to be team players.

> —SUSIE WALTON
> SAN DIEGO, CALIFORNIA
> 😊 28 😊 26 😊 24 😊 22

TEEN TOPIC

American children and teens spend about 7.5 more hours a week at school and doing homework than children and teens did 20 years ago.

PREPARING FOR COLLEGE

EVERY PARENT I KNOW HAS GONE NUTS at college application time. Their kids seemed uninterested, they procrastinated, and they took little responsibility for the process. It was impossible to believe that they would get it together and actually apply before the deadline. Somehow, the kids all got through it and got into colleges they like. I think the kids were dragging their feet because it was so scary to think of going away.

> —S.S.
> *SARATOGA SPRINGS, NEW YORK*
> 22

. . . .

LET YOUR CHILD VISIT AS MANY COLLEGES AS POSSIBLE. They can make a much more informed choice once they have actually spent some time on the campuses. As a parent you should give your opinion about where they go but the choice has to be theirs. I wouldn't have chosen the school my daughter is attending but she loves it and is doing very well—and that's the bottom line.

> —M.E.S.
> *CARNEGIE, PENNSYLVANIA*
> 21

. . . .

EVEN IF YOUR KID IS ATTENDING A SCHOOL close to home, encourage them to live on campus. It's the first step toward getting them out of the nest once and for all.

> —J.J.
> *BULGER, PENNSYLVANIA*
> 17

. . . .

ENCOURAGE THEM TO TAKE A VARIETY OF CLASSES during their freshman year. Even kids who think they know what they want to do can have a change of heart and find something they like even better if they have a wide variety of experiences.

> —B.G.
> *PITTSBURGH, PENNSYLVANIA*
> 24

NEVER SAY, "YOU COULD HAVE DONE BETTER!"
to your teenager. I said that to my son after he
scored very low on a test that he should have
aced. He was already disappointed in himself for
his performance, but saying that he could have
done better really hurt him. I'll never forget the
look on his face. Now I make sure, before I say a
negative comment, that I say two positive comments. It works great! Remember: Two positives
before a negative.

—*LEIGH DOBSON*
TORONTO, ONTARIO, CANADA
😊 *25* 😊 *24*

• • • • • • • • •

A LOT OF PARENTS THREATEN TO PULL their kids
out of sports if their grades go down: I think this
is a mistake. My son hated school, but he loved
football. In order maintain eligibility, the school
required him to have at least a C average. He
actually ended up graduating with a C+/B-
average. I'm convinced this wouldn't have
happened without football. His coach got on
him harder than his dad or I did.

—*BARB ZAHN*
FRANKTOWN, COLORADO
😊 *47* 😊 *46* 😊 *45*

• • • • • • • • •

I WASN'T VERY POPULAR WITH their coaches
because when they didn't do well in school I
restricted them from sports. One of their coaches
called to yell at me and told me I was the worst
mother he had ever seen. But I would do
it the same way today—I didn't have
any other way to get them to do their
school work.

—*DEEDEE MELMET*
SONOMA, CALIFORNIA
😊 *35* 😊 *32* 😊 *30* 😊 *28*

TEEN TOPIC

In 2004,
almost half—
48 percent—of
all graduating
high school
students took
the SAT. The
average verbal
score was 508,
while the
average math
score was 518.

EXTRA CREDIT?

KIDS SHOULD GET INVOLVED IN SCHOOL ACTIVITIES. Pick your thing: If you don't want sports, be in the theater. The kids who are successful in school are involved in school. One of my sons was involved in sports every season. My other son was a pretty good athlete but he didn't like it much. I made him do something. One semester, he ran cross-country; another he did theater.

> —*CAREN MASEM*
> *GREENSBORO, NORTH CAROLINA*
> 🙂33 🙂28

. . . .

IF YOU'RE A LITTLE WORRIED ABOUT YOUR KIDS' GRADES, encourage them to join some after-school activity or sports team. It seems counterintuitive, but a lot of the teams have requirements that the kids keep their grades up, and staying on a team they love can be a huge motivator. And, from my own experience, I've found that sometimes if your days are more structured, you actually become more efficient.

> —*S.M.P.*
> *PORTLAND, MAINE*
> 🙂12 🙂8

. . . .

LIMIT EXTRACURRICULAR ACTIVITIES IF YOU HAVE TO. I don't allow my teenager to participate in sports in the first semester of a school year. He needs that time to adjust to the new teacher, to learn what's expected of him, and to settle back into school.

> —*DEB UHLER*
> *HELLERTOWN, PENNSYLVANIA*
> 🙂14 🙂10

MY SON IS IN THE GIFTED/TALENTED CATEGORY and finds most regular school subjects pretty boring. School basically "sucks," except art and photography and music. So support the continuation of art and music in your school curriculum!

—*J.S.*
HOUSTON, TEXAS
18

. . . .

I BELIEVE THAT ORGANIZED SPORTS can teach valuable life lessons to kids during their formative years. The camaraderie, and being part of a team, taught me so much in high school. No classroom learning can replace those lessons. Parents should encourage kids to find a sport they love to play, and to play it to the best of their abilities. They will learn things that they will take with them for the rest of their lives. And if they are good enough they might even earn a college scholarship and make things easier on their parents financially.

—*MITZIE HAGEN*
WHEELING, WEST VIRGINIA
15

. . . .

MY DAUGHTER GOT INTO SWIMMING AT SEVEN YEARS OLD, and it was so demanding. By high school she'd have practice every day for several hours; it consumed all her time. But looking at the pros versus the cons, it worked out. And I shut up after a while. You have to remember that it's about her and not about you.

—*HERB GRIFFITH*
FISHERSVILLE, VIRGINIA
33 31

I let my house be a place where my daughter's friends came with their friends. She would not have told me what was going on, but her friends would.

—*Pat Williams*
Atlanta, Georgia
21 19

I THINK FOOTBALL IS A GREAT EXTRACURRICULAR activity for teens. You don't just learn the sport. It teaches life lessons—how to work as a team, where you fit in, discipline, how to do your part for the big picture. My son has been successful all of his sports life, until this past year. His senior year his two best friends, whom he grew up with and played football with since he was 10, left for another high school. My son didn't want to leave the school. It hurt him when his two friends left. It felt like they were walking out on him. He had to deal with that and with the fact that their departure from the football team brought more expectations of him. It taught my son that things can happen and you have to persevere. In hindsight it will turn out to be a very good thing for my son.

—*Gary Collins*
Tampa, Florida
17

• • • • • • • •

YOU HAVE TO LET YOUR KIDS MAKE their own mistakes sometimes. My daughter quit dance when she was 13, and I knew she would regret it. I tried to talk her out of it, but it just made her more adamant. After a couple of years she went back to it, and now she is more dedicated than ever, because she was allowed to see the consequences of her own actions. It was very frustrating to see her do something I knew she would regret, but that was a lesson she had to learn on her own.

—*Grace*
Chapel Hill, North Carolina
22 19 15

Getting Social: On Friends, Groups, & the Opposite Sex

or most teens, friends are not the most important part of their lives—they're the only important part! Friends—yes, those weirdos slumped on your sofa—exert a powerful influence on your teen, so hope your child will choose them wisely, and help if you can.

I USED TO TELL MY TEENAGE SON to bring his friends to the house. If you know the friends you know your child. I would make them lunch and see with whom I'm dealing. Some of them had crazy hair and earrings, but they went to Harvard and good colleges. Every age has a different craziness.

—BATIA ELKAYAM
LOS ANGELES, CALIFORNIA

ALWAYS KNOW WHO THEY ARE WITH AND WHAT THEY ARE DOING— WITHIN REASON.

—PAGET PERRAULT
MELBOURNE,
AUSTRALIA
35 30

MAKE YOUR HOUSE THE HANGOUT. I always wanted my house to be the hangout because I couldn't know what my kids were doing at their friends' houses. You can't necessarily pick their friends for them when they get older, but at least you'll know who they're with if they're at your house.

—*SUE G.*
LYNCOURT, NEW YORK
21 18 14

• • • • • • • •

"It only takes one bad friend to change the foundation you've made, so you should know what your child is doing every single day and who they are hanging out with."

—*ANONYMOUS*
LAKE FOREST, ILLINOIS
17 14 10 8

• • • • • • • •

EACH OF OUR CHILDREN HAS HAD a friend at some time that worried us. However, we made a point to actively get to know the friend. It showed that we cared about what happened to our child, and it showed the friend that there was a friendly home to visit. It kept our son grounded while around another child who probably wasn't.

—*C. HOPE CLARK*
PHOENIX, ARIZONA
31 26 21 19

GET A REALLY BIG VEHICLE and offer to be the chauffeur whenever they and a group of their friends need one. They tend to view you as part of the inside of the car. Fade the speakers to the back so the music is louder there, and they'll talk louder. Then just listen. You'll be amazed at what you find out—who got suspended, who's going out with whom, who came to school dressed like a slut. Whatever you do, don't participate in the conversation or they'll know you're listening and shut up.

> —*PAT CURRY*
> *ATHENS, GEORGIA*
> 👧 17 👧 15

• • • • • • • •

WE MADE SURE WE KNEW where our kids were, and we kept track of their friends. We made sure they had decent ones. We told them they had to respect the law and respect other people's property. They did pull some stuff, but nothing ever too bad. They knew what we expected from them.

> —*ANONYMOUS*
> *MASON, MICHIGAN*
> 😀 48 😀 46 😀 45 😀 44 😀 42 👧 40

• • • • • • • •

A MAJOR CONCERN FOR PARENTS IS over what happens when a teen is pressured by friends or groups. I advise parents to prepare their kids for the pressure by having rehearsals at home. Pretend to be your teen's friend and say, "Why don't you smoke this?" Encourage your teen to come up with strong responses that he is comfortable with, such as, "Gee, I wish I could but I have such a strict mom" or "I would, but the coach would kick me off the team."

> *ERIKA KARRES*
> *CHAPEL HILL, NORTH CAROLINA*
> *DAUGHTERS IN THEIR LATE 30S*

Make your home the gathering point, regardless of how many soft drinks and chips you have to buy. Then you'll know where your kids are.

> —*ELAINE FANTLE*
> *SHIMBERG*
> *TAMPA, FLORIDA*
> 👧 41 😀 40 👧 38
> 😀 37 😀 32

LEAVING THE PROBLEM BEHIND

At about 14, my son started hanging out with kids I called "the jerky boys"—no ambition other than to quit school at 16, get a girlfriend, get a job at Grease Monkey, and get a car. They hung out at the mall and the bus station, smoking and trying to be cool. Solution? He finished middle school at his dad and step-mom's in Maine. They live on the fringes of a very, very small town with a regional middle school and high school. He had to be on a school bus, and couldn't just wander downtown and hang out. He got into a parochial high school in Denver, which would have meant another commute, so he pleaded to go to the local public high school. I said, "Get your grades up, or the next choice of schools is mine." He didn't, and he ended up going to boarding school in New Hampshire.

—C.W.
BOULDER, COLORADO
22

WHEN MY WIFE AND I ARE HOME on the weekend, we allow the kids to have their friends over to hang out in the basement. I generally check in on them to make sure they're not visibly smoking pot or something. But that's my own overprotectiveness. They're good kids: if they're in the house, they'll play by house rules. I guess the parties occur when parents are not around.

—*JASON B.*
SAN FRANCISCO, CALIFORNIA
19 14

• • • • • • • •

If you're looking for information, ask your teens questions that don't have single-word answers.

—*KIM JAFFE*
REDMOND,
WASHINGTON
43 40 36
34 32

WE OPEN OUR HOUSE TO OUR KIDS' FRIENDS. If their friends are over, we treat them like part of the family while they're in the house. That way, my wife and I can establish a relationship with them and be able to talk. This worked with one of my son's friends: We had him over a lot and were comfortable talking to him. My wife and I knew he did a lot of drugs, but we felt comfortable enough to bring it up with this kid and ask if he could refrain from involving our son.

—*V.P.*
MUNDELEIN, ILLINOIS
21 18 15 12 7 5

• • • • • • • •

I THINK TRYING TO STEER YOUR KIDS away from kids who you think may be a problem is a bad idea. It will just drive them together. You have to let your kids make their own mistakes and learn from them, and hanging out with the wrong kids can teach lessons, too.

—*MATT MARSHALL*
EVANS CITY, PENNSYLVANIA
14

TALK TO YOUR TEENAGER and get to know their friends: welcome them into your home. The more you see and relate to teenagers, the safer you'll feel—even if it's a false sense of safe.

—*JANIS BLAISE*
DIABLO, CALIFORNIA
25

• • • • • • • •

   "Accept your teen's friends for who they are. Don't put them down; it's like telling your teen he or she has poor taste. Remember, they're trying to figure things out. They don't need parents criticizing every choice they make."

—*GRACE*
LIVERPOOL, NEW YORK
17 15

• • • • • • • •

ONE OF THE BEST WAYS TO KNOW your kid's friends is to make your home an open house. From when our kids were in kindergarten right up through high school, there was hardly ever a weekend when we didn't have a number of kids over at our house.

—*ANONYMOUS*
SAN FRANCISCO, CALIFORNIA
21 16

I WORK HARD AT LIKING MY DAUGHTER'S FRIENDS: she has chosen them and my positive reaction to them is a way of honoring her choices. If I genuinely do not like a friend, I will not say this directly. What I do is let my daughter know some of my reservations. I find that my observations are often shared by my daughter, although she says positive things about her friend that I may not have seen. My child seems very good at weighing all of this and choosing her friends well.

> —BRENDA KILGORE
> PHOENIX, CANBERRA, AUSTRALIAN CAPITAL TERRITORY,
> AUSTRALIA
> 🐣15

THE HE-MAN WOMAN-HATER'S CLUB

My most vivid memory of my son's teenage years was when he and his mates were in the lounge-room, and I was in the kitchen chopping up some veggies. The way he and his friends, most of whom had professional women as mothers, were talking about women . . . I had a carving knife in my hand, and I thought that what I should do was march into the living room and stab them all. I didn't; I thought that was very good of me. You have to realize that so much of this is just testosterone. And you know, I don't think any of them meant it. There are huge biological things going on and you just have to contain yourself while it's happening.

> —MEL MILLER
> BRISBANE, QUEENSLAND, AUSTRALIA
> 😊23 🐣9

Let them make their home a place where their friends can come to congregate. That way you'll know where they are.

—*Isabel*
Berkeley Heights,
New Jersey

My 17-year-old daughter recently had a situation at school where one of her friends changed dramatically over a few months. My daughter came to talk to me about it. I could see her friend's behavior was bothering her too much to let it go. I suggested that my daughter talk to a counselor at school. Without indicating who talked to her, the counselor initiated a conversation with my daughter's friends, and the situation improved.

—*Anonymous*
New Jersey
17   14

• • • • • • • •

Help your teens choose friends wisely. I told my kids three things. First, choose friends who love you for who you are and don't ask you to change. Second, make sure that being with your friends makes you happy. If a relationship doesn't make you happy, question it. And third, know that there's a reason for the adage, "Show me your friends, and I'll show you what kind of person you are." My wife and I have been careful to teach this by example.

—*Al Parisi*
Agoura Hills, California
21   16

• • • • • • • •

My father always said, "You are who you hang around with." So I'm afraid that thought process stays with me as I evaluate my son's friends. I would definitely like him to find some friends who find school more important. His current friends are a little lazier than I would prefer. But, in general, I think they are goodhearted kids, and not a bad threat.

—*Toby Lynn*
Atlanta, Georgia
14

DON'T GIVE YOUR TEENS MORE MONEY than they need—especially when they're going out with friends. It doesn't make them look good in the eyes of their friends; their friends will only be jealous. Their friends' parents won't appreciate it, either.

—*H.S.*
GOLDEN, COLORADO
 *14* *12*

* * * * * * * *

"I thought my teenage son was hanging out with weirdos. Now most of those weirdos have graduated from great colleges and are working on advanced degrees. "

—*L.M.*
FALMOUTH, MAINE
35 *35* *29* *23*

* * * * * * * *

MY DAUGHTER WAS ABOUT 12, and her friends were changing at the time. I was picking her up when I saw her girlfriend kiss a boy goodbye. I said I didn't like that, and I didn't like the clothes her friend was wearing, either. Then I asked, "Why do you want to be friends with her? You're not like that." That hurt my daughter a lot. Eventually, on her own, she became uncomfortable with her friends because she realized they were changing in a way she didn't like. It had to be her choice, not mine.

—*GRACE*
LIVERPOOL, NEW YORK
17 *15*

NOT JUST TALK, REAL DIVERSITY

Seventy-nine percent of teens count among their friends someone of a different race, religion, or sexual orientation.

IT'S IMPORTANT TO GET GREAT MENTORS for your children. They can be older teens or maybe someone just starting college. Pick young men or women you respect. It won't just happen; you've got to encourage the relationship. For several years, my son has had a great relationship with a young man who plays on the Syracuse University basketball team. That gave my son someone to talk to about things he didn't want to talk to my wife and me about. We had his mentor over for dinner. We took our son to his place. I would talk to the young man about what he saw in my son. It's given my son the confidence to pick the right kinds of friends.

—*BRINTON*
LIVERPOOL, NEW YORK
😊 *17* 👧 *15*

TTYL: Talking with Teens

Teens are all about communicating, at least when it involves using the latest techno-gizmos to do it. But communicating with parents can resemble parallel tracks. Moms and dads talk, lecture, yell, cajole, and explain; in response, teens grunt, grumble, yell, mutter, and clam up. Where's the common ground? What's the solution? The magic word is Listen. As savvy parents explain in this chapter, you can learn a lot from listening. Read on, and keep your ears open.

LISTEN TO YOUR KIDS. That means *really* listen, with eye contact; this helps you respond relevantly and insightfully to the matter raised.

—ARCH
LONDONDERRY, VERMONT
18 14

TALKING TO KIDS DOESN'T MEAN *YOU* ARE TALKING— YOU'RE LISTENING.

—F.M.
LONG BRANCH, NEW JERSEY
28 25

Remember that their hormones rule and try to be patient. This too shall pass.

—*A.N.P.*
Pittsburgh,
Pennsylvania

NEVER PASS UP THE CHANCE to let your teenager know that you are proud of him. Whether it's for the A they got on their last history test, or because they made the Honor Roll, or just for actually doing their chores, teenagers like to hear compliments and know their parents care. They like to get praise for the good things they do, even if it's only every so often that they do good things.

—*Sara Sterling*
Barling, Arizona
Former teenager

• • • • • • • •

TELLING YOUR KIDS TO BE QUIET is effective until kids get to be about 10 or 11. After that, try "Can I say something?" This is how I would speak to my kids, and it worked well. Sometimes they would be rude and reply, "No!" When that happens, let them fume, then get on with your point.

—*Emmillio E.*
Vancouver, Canada
27   22

• • • • • • • •

ONE NIGHT OUR SON SAID TO ME, "How come you never believe me when I tell you things? You always ask me all these questions." I said, "I teach high school. I spend all day around kids who say, 'You wouldn't believe how dumb my parents are. I said so and so, and they believed me.'" I taught for 31 years. Parents want to believe their kids are open with them. That's just not the case, as I've ascertained. Parents need to be very careful and ask lots of questions. Your kids will tell you what you want to hear, and it'll sound very believable. With my students there was definitely this attitude that if you smile and say the right thing, it'll be OK.

—*B. Mills*
Hillsboro, Oregon
39   36   34

COMMUNICATION EQUALS SURVIVAL! We parents think we are talking to a brick wall, but be persistent. My daughter had a real self-esteem problem and went through a period of time where she would withdraw from everyone, be angry one minute and crying the next. I spent a lot of time talking to her about my teenage years, telling her that I remember feeling the same things she was feeling. And I encouraged her to talk to her friends about some of these feelings, as I was sure she would discover that they were going through the same things.

—*N.S.*
TAMPA, FLORIDA
🐶 *41* 🐾 *36*

* * * * * * * *

❝ If what your child is asking isn't dangerous, cost prohibitive, or illegal, give them your opinion and then let them decide. But if it *is* dangerous, cost prohibitive, or illegal, just say no. ❞

—*JEFFREY SMITH*
HARMONY, PENNSYLVANIA
🐶 *20* 🐾 *19* 🐾 *17* 🐶 *17* 🐾 *15* 🐶 *13*

* * * * * * * *

HE TELLS ME HE HATES ME. I do something and he says, "That's why I hate you." It's just part of the process of pulling away. I say, "If you're going to be mean to me, you're never going to drive; so there."

—*DANIEL*
ATLANTA, GEORGIA
🐾 *14* 🐾 *12* 🐾 *5*

TEEN LINGO DECODED

IF IT SOUNDS NEGATIVE, IT IS POSITIVE. Example: "tight," which is normally used in a sentence like, "My pants are too tight." "Tight" actually means "really good"—as in, "That party was tight!"

Sometimes the word or phrase actually varies slightly from its English origins. Example: "true dat," as in the response, "True dat, dog." This is an affirmation of what someone else just said, and means, "That is true, my friend."

> —*SHELLEY*
> *TAMPA, FLORIDA*
> 😊 *17* 😊 *12*

• • • • • • • •

MY SON HAS BEEN SAYING, "Spot on" lately. I didn't know he was British. I guess it means "right on."

> —*ANGELA HENNESSEY*
> 😊 *12* 😊 *8*

• • • • • • • •

"Fa Shizzle": for sure
"Crunk": crazy drunk
"I hit that": I had sex with that person
"Get blowed": smoke weed
"Let's bounce": let's leave

> —*ROD ENGLISH, 19*
> *AURORA, COLORADO*

• • • • • • • •

"Baller": basketball player
"Hottie": sexy guy or girl
"Are you trippin'?": Are you kidding, are you crazy?
"Get it crunkin'": get it started, e.g. "Get the party crunkin'!"
"Dis": disrespect, make fun of
"Whack": messed up, weird
"Shut up": get out of here, you're exaggerating or kidding

> —*CONNIE PROULX*
> 😊 *15* 😊 *12*

THE FIRST TIME MY FATHER TOLD ME HE LOVED ME
was at my wedding, when I was 30. I do the
180-degree opposite with my son. I hug him
15 times a day. I tell him I love him every time I
see him. In front of his friends, he will openly hug
me and kiss my cheek and say, "I love you, Pop,"
and he's not afraid to show his emotions.

—*GARY COLLINS*
TAMPA, FLORIDA
17

If you get upset, walk away.

—*NANCY*
NICEVILLE, FLORIDA
17

MY ADVICE TO PARENTS WITH TEENAGERS is to sit
down and listen to them—visit with them as you
do your friends or older family members. They do
want to talk and tell you what is going on in their
lives. They have their own minds and they really
want to be loved, respected and listened to.

—*S. SALMON*
MUSKOGEE, OKLAHOMA
15 13

WHENEVER MY SONS AND I WOULD ARGUE, instead
of yelling back at them I'd simply say, "I'm going
to stay on the high road here." It was a very effective technique because I didn't have to lower
myself to their behavior: I waited for them to
calm down before I would actually talk to them.
They'd get mad at my non-responses,
but it usually worked.

—*L.A.*
CLEVELAND, OHIO
23 21

SOMETIMES MY DAUGHTER is particularly close-minded about some subjects, including boys, friends and music. She has an argumentative side, so she'll argue with us just for practice. She'll argue about the most absurd things. Recently, we argued about something we would generally agree on. I wish she'd have a little more respect for the experiences of those older than she; I think she'd appreciate it in the long run.

—*JERRY*
EAST NORTHPORT, NEW YORK
🐵 *16* 😊 *2*

• • • • • • • •

Listen, especially when you have them trapped in the car with you. Keep the radio off and your mouth shut.

—*ELAINE FANTLE SHIMBERG*
TAMPA, FLORIDA
🐵 *41* 😊 *40* 🐵 *38*
😊 *37* 😊 *32*

IF YOUR KID IS SULLEN OR UNRESPONSIVE, teasing is a very effective tool. Part of the wall you have to break down is when they take themselves too seriously. If you can tease your kids in a loving way, make them see the humor in the situation, it can really help get you through some tough times. And it can teach them that a sense of humor about oneself is indispensable in life.

—*BRENDA*
CHARLESTON, WEST VIRGINIA
🐵 *30* 😊 *22*

• • • • • • • •

THE PHRASE MY WIFE AND I USED in response to arguments like, "But Johnny's allowed to do it!" was "I don't care if they're standing in line to (fill in the blank). You're not going to." I'd definitely recommend coming up with your own blanket phrase that both you and your spouse use consistently. There are two benefits to doing this: After the kids hear it a couple of times, they'll know you're serious. And, they can't play Mom's and Dad's responses against each other, because you're both saying the same thing.

—*JOE HOLLIMAN*
CENTENNIAL, COLORADO
🐵 *29* 😊 *27*

TALK AROUND THE CLOCK

DON'T JUST TRY TO TALK TO YOUR TEEN between 7 and 7:30 a.m. before school each day. Talk to your teenager by e-mail. Put little notes under his pillow at night. Hang a bulletin board in your teen's bathroom, and tack up articles that you think he'll enjoy and notes from you. Talk to your kids in the car, when you're driving them to and from school.

> —*ERIKA KARRES*
> *CHAPEL HILL, NORTH CAROLINA*
> *DAUGHTERS IN THEIR LATE 30S*

• • • • • • • • •

THEY KNOW MY DOOR IS ALWAYS OPEN. My son never felt like talking to me during daylight hours, or even before my bedtime. But he would come into my room at 2 a.m., sit next to me on the bed, and say, "Mom, are you awake? I need to talk with you about something." I'd say, "Sure, what is it?" And we would have our best talks in the middle of the night. I never said no when he wanted to talk. My son still calls sometimes late at night to talk, although now that he's an adult we've asked him to make it before 11 p.m. But he's really comfortable calling and saying "Mom, I have girl problems," or whatever he needs to talk about.

> —*ANONYMOUS*
> *WAKEFIELD, NEW HAMPSHIRE*
> 🌼26 🌼17

• • • • • • • • •

WHEN YOUR CHILD WANTS TO TALK, give her your full and complete attention. Put down the book or whatever you're doing, and be 'all ears'—no facial expressions, no clucks, sighs, moans, or 'oh, no's.' Don't let her infer a negative judgment on what she's saying; save that for when she's finished.

> —*N.*
> *BROOKLYN, NEW YORK*
> 🌼17

MY OLDER SON GOT IN TROUBLE AT SCHOOL. It was hard not to freak out, but we thought it was more important to talk rather than mandate, to keep the dialogue open; to doggedly ask the same questions over and over. Sometimes you don't want to hear the answers, but keep asking. "Where were you? Who were you with? What did you do?" I can't tell you how many late-night conversations I had like this with my boys. I would go to work bleary-eyed in the morning.

—*F.M.*
LONG BRANCH, NEW JERSEY
28 25

· · · · · · · ·

 Sometimes my kids say I ask too many questions. But I say, 'It's my right as a parent.'

—*DUANE STONE*
MIAMI, FLORIDA
24 18

· · · · · · · ·

ONE QUESTION PARENTS ASK over and over is, "How can I be a good parent in the two minutes I have left each day?" Instead of fighting, my son and I recently found a much more productive way to deal with our anger: we take a timeout and write each other letters. It's calming and reassuring, because it gives us both the chance to organize our thoughts and say what we really mean.

—*ROBYN MURAMOTO*
CENTENNIAL, COLORADO
15 13

EXPLAIN TO TEENS *WHY* you want them to do something, and be honest with yourself as well as your kids. For example, a mom in the parenting class I teach came to me and said she was having a struggle with her son, who wanted to be out with his friends every night. I asked her why this bothered her. "Because he needs to rest," she said. I asked her "why" a few more times, trying to get to the real heart of the issue. "Because I miss him," she said, finally. "Did you ever tell *him* that?" I asked. She admitted that she hadn't, and I suggested that maybe telling him *why* she really wanted him to be home would be a powerful motivator.

> —SUSIE WALTON
> SAN DIEGO, CALIFORNIA
> 😊 28 😊 26 😊 24 😊 22

TEEN TOPIC

In a survey from the 1990s, 50 percent of teen respondents said they trust their parents most for reliable and complete information about birth control, while only 12 percent preferred a friend.

. . . .

THE BIGGEST FIGHTS I'VE HAD with my teens are when they feel misunderstood. It's hard to do, but try to slow down and understand what they are feeling. The issue will be resolved faster, and with less pain.

> —ANNE SMALLEY
> WOODBURY, NEW JERSEY
> 👧 19 👧 15

. . . .

ASSUME THEY'RE GOING TO LIE TO YOU. I had three teenagers, and I asked one of them if she had gone to school. She said yes, but when I called the school, they had no record of her being in class. When I confronted her about it, she said, "You asked me if I went to school: I did. But I didn't say I went to *class*."

> —KEN D.
> ATLANTA, GEORGIA
> 👦 45 👦 41 👦 34

THE BIG TALKS

YOU CAN'T AVOID AWKWARDNESS WITH BIG TALKS. Tell him at the
beginning, "You're going to hate this, but I don't care. This is
important. You have to listen to me. I'll keep it as short as
possible." Then *keep* it short. Give up on the idea of it being a
warm, interactive event. Know in advance what the critical things
are that you want to communicate and do it quickly while he sulks
and avoids eye contact. Don't insist on a response.

> —*S.S.*
> *SARATOGA SPRINGS, NEW YORK*
> 22

• • • • • • • • •

I JUST PLUNGE IN. I've reviewed the facts and given them some
scary stats. I wanted them to know that oral sex can give them
STDs, too, and that it could leave them with a
lifetime of misery in the form of herpes. I also
talked about the responsibility of being a
parent. I always talk about safe sex, including
words along the lines of, "I am not saying I think
it's OK, but if you decide to have sex make it safe sex . . . "

> —*BARB*
> *LOUISVILLE, KENTUCKY*
> 16 15 8

• • • • • • • • •

ONE EVENING WHEN MY DAUGHTER WAS 16 I asked her straight out
about drugs. She just looked at me for a minute and said, "What
happened to 'Don't ask, don't tell?'"

> —*N.*
> *BROOKLYN, NEW YORK*
> 17

YOU HAVE TO BE REALLY OPEN to your kids and not let anything shock you. When your teen does tell you the truth, you shouldn't overreact.

—*J.R.*
CHICAGO, ILLINOIS
21 18

• • • • • • • •

I DID ALL I COULD TO MAINTAIN a close relationship with my children through the teenage years. Because of our relationship, my children were comfortable enough to talk to me about anything that was going on in their worlds. I knew that I had been successful in keeping the lines of communication open when, as a senior in high school, my son asked my permission to ditch school on annual Ditch Day.

—*W.F.R.M.*
OKLAHOMA CITY, OKLAHOMA
35 31

• • • • • • • •

I NEVER HAD A MAJOR ISSUE with my daughter because I treated her like an adult. People forget what it is like to be a teen: You don't feel much different than your parents. Teens have valid ideas and opinions and shouldn't be treated like they don't.

—*ALME BLAIR*
NEW YORK, NEW YORK
17

• • • • • • • •

LISTEN! **DON'T OFFER ADVICE,** don't tell them how you handled your emotions, don't try to solve the problems. Just listen. Remember, they are going through the same emotional things we went through, but with different pressures and a different society than we had growing up.

—*RITA PORTER*
SPRINGFIELD, MISSOURI
14

Ask your teens lots of questions, because they know everything.

—*DUANE STONE*
MIAMI, FLORIDA
24 18

Talk about responsibility and integrity, and live what you preach.

—*Vickie Simpson*
Aptos, California
35

Be realistic. This is life, not a sitcom. Kids are messy, they stay up too late, they don't do their homework, they lose things, they forget those arrangements which are important to you but not to them, they don't practice the instruments you've spent money on. My biggest parenting failure was about my son practicing the violin. I lost perspective and we battled constantly. One day as I was stewing over it, it suddenly hit me that I had created World War III over *practicing*, for Pete's sake. When I was a teen I never practiced, either. I stopped nagging and he probably practiced more—he certainly didn't practice any less—and we got along much better.

—*S.S.*
Saratoga Springs, New York
22

• • • • • • • •

I learned how to appeal to them. If it is my son, I talk sports and find out what he is interested in. My daughter is emotional so we speak about warm and fuzzy and deep things. Your parenting must adapt to the kid rather than the other way around. Whatever you do, do *not* be sarcastic. They will toss it back at you.

—*Yehuda*
Camden, New Jersey

• • • • • • • •

With your teens, you can't lose touch with them, even a little. It could mean waking up one morning to find your kid has a coke addiction or an STD. I am always aware of where my kids are, whom they are with, and what time they'll be home. I will even sit down and have conversations with their friends. You learn a lot that way.

—*Frances Cisneros Jenks*
San Antonio, Texas
17

LUNCHTIME ADVICE

Try communicating with your teens in writing, especially on tough issues. This gives you the chance to really think about what you want to say without being too emotional or confrontational. Review what you write at least twice before you give it to your teenager.

One night when my daughter was a sophomore in high school, a group of her friends were at our house. None of the girls had siblings, so these friends were like sisters to each other. And, that night, a sibling rivalry broke out. I overheard some mean-spirited things being said.

In the past, I had tucked small notes inside my daughter's lunch bag, but for some reason that next morning I wrote a note right on the outside of the bag. I wrote that friends might make unkind remarks but that you shouldn't let those remarks get you down. Most often these words are spoken out of frustration and/or jealousy. They are not a true reflection of you. My daughter read the note that day at lunch and quickly discarded the bag.

I wrote a new note to my daughter each day after that. She began to be less discreet in reading them and her friends soon wanted to read the notes, too. My daughter told me what happened and I said, "I guess you don't want me to write them anymore." "Oh, no," she said, "I just wanted to let you know that you have a broader audience now."

I communicated lots of important things to my daughter, and her friends, through those little notes. They were cheap brown paper bags; the messages written on them, however, were timeless and priceless.

—AL PARISI
AGOURA HILLS, CALIFORNIA
🐾21 ⚙16

I talk to them as if I was a teenager, too. This is very important. I give constant reminders that I, too, was a kid. I build trust and listen.

—*PAUL REYES*
PUERTO RICO

REMEMBER THAT YOU, TOO, HATED IT when your parents asked annoying questions like, "Where did you go tonight?" or "Who'd you go with?" or "Did you have fun?" or "Why didn't you take the trash out before you left?" If you don't ask them *any* questions, they'll wonder what the hell is wrong with you and tell you everything you ever wanted to know.

—*CASSANDRA FOX*
FAIRFAX STATION, VIRGINIA
18 15

• • • • • • • •

WHEN A CHILD ASKS QUESTIONS, you don't dictate to him. I'd give him options. I'd say, "Son, I'm not going to dictate to you. You'll have to make a choice." Then, I'd suggest the options.

—*PEDRO RAMIREZ JR.*
AUSTIN, TEXAS
34

• • • • • • • •

WHEN MY DAUGHTER WAS IN NINTH GRADE, she was having a bad week, so her mother and I sent flowers to her school along with a card that read, "I hope your day gets better." It showed her we cared and were there to help her. Many times, if you don't back up the words "I love you" with an action, it's too easy for teenagers to forget.

—*JOHN COOKE*
GREELEY, COLORADO
23 21

• • • • • • • •

TEENAGERS HAVE A GIFT FOR STARTING ARGUMENTS over semantics and if you get wrapped up in that, you won't get anywhere. You have to stay calm and stay on the subject matter at hand.

—*JANE*
BROOKLYN, NEW YORK
16 2

THE HARDEST THING IS LEARNING TO LISTEN to your child. My daughter tells me that whenever she shares something with me I criticize her. I tell her how she should have done something instead of just listening. Unless they're telling you something that's really a crazy situation, it's OK to not direct or do something.

—CINDY STEVENS
SAN DIEGO, CALIFORNIA
14

. . . .

6 Talk to them about sex, drugs, and rock 'n' roll. Let them know that no subject is taboo. 99

—CARMEN TURNER
NEW YORK, NEW YORK
15 13

. . . .

DURING MY DAUGHTER'S FIRST WEEK of high school, she told me about an incident she had with one of her teachers, who she said was mean. My immediate response was to blame my daughter for not getting along with her teacher and criticize her for saying mean things. After reflecting on our conversation, which ended with my daughter in tears, I realize I should have listened to the incident sympathetically and suggested ways in which she might give her teacher the benefit of the doubt. In retrospect, I should feel lucky that she chose to share the incident with me at all.

—H.S.
GOLDEN, COLORADO
14 12

THE WORST THING MY TEEN EVER SAID TO ME

MY ELDEST SON AND I ONCE GOT INTO A HUGE FIGHT about his failing grades in some of his college courses and he said no matter what he did he knew he would end up more successful than me. I dropped out of college in my junior year and it keeps coming back to haunt me now as I try to get my kids prepared for college. My son later apologized for saying it, but it's something I never forgot.

> —TIM LAKE
> BADEN, PENNSYLVANIA
> 21 16 13

• • • • • • • •

MY DAUGHTER WOULD OPEN HER DOOR AND SCREAM, "I hate you, Mom!" And then she would close the door and open it up and shout out her stepfather's name and say, "And I hate you too!"

> —P.W.
> ATLANTA, GEORGIA
> 21 19

• • • • • • • •

I WAS IN THE BATHROOM BRUSHING MY HAIR and my 16-year-old daughter said, with a snarl: "Do you have to breathe that way?"

> —ANONYMOUS
> IOWA CITY, IOWA
> 35

• • • • • • • •

YOU DON'T LOVE ME—all you care about is how much things cost!

> —K.
> SOUTHFIELD, CONNECTICUT
> 17 13

• • • • • • • •

YOU'VE RUINED MY LIFE!

> —N.
> BROOKLYN, NEW YORK
> 17

IT'S ALL YOUR FAULT!

—*S.K.*
SEATTLE, WASHINGTON
33 32

. . . .

I CAN'T WAIT TO GET OUT OF HERE so I'll never have to deal with you again.

—*ANONYMOUS*
BROOKLYN, NEW YORK
23 16

. . . .

I HAVE NO FRIENDS because I have a terrible personality that I inherited from you!

—*ANONYMOUS*
ASTORIA, NEW YORK
17

. . . .

YOU DON'T WANT ME TO BE HAPPY!

—*ANONYMOUS*
NORTHAMPTON, MASSACHUSETTS
15 13

. . . .

I WISH YOU WEREN'T MY PARENTS!

—*ANONYMOUS*
GLEN RIDGE, NEW JERSEY
20

. . . .

I'M CALLING THE COPS ON YOU!

—*ANONYMOUS*
PLAINFIELD, MASSACHUSETTS
30 26

MY DAUGHTER IS 14 YEARS OLD, going on 21. We're constantly butting heads over things. She wants to do this and she wants to do that. And she comes up with valid points sometimes. But I resort to, "I'm the mom and I said no." She has a good case, but that doesn't mean I'm going to give in. She might be mad at me at that moment, but she'll understand later.

　　　　—CINDY STEVENS
　　　　SAN DIEGO, CALIFORNIA
　　　　🐶 14

• • • • • • • •

“ If you aren't overly strict or naïve, your teen will open up and tell you things. The best thing is not to be judgmental, but to be positive and accepting. ”

　　—ANONYMOUS
　　CHICAGO, ILLINOIS
　　🐶 24 🐶 20 👶 19 👶 17 🐶 15

• • • • • • • •

WE TOOK OUR BOYS CAMPING and fishing in the summer, and skiing in the winter. Obviously, these are fun activities, but there was a hidden benefit: When you're sitting around a campfire or on a chairlift, that's a great time to carry on a conversation about drugs or sex because you know you have a captive audience. If he is feeling uncomfortable, he can't just slip off to his room.

　　　　—JOAN K. HITCHENS
　　　　CENTENNIAL, COLORADO
　　　　👶 32 👶 28

DEALING WITH TEEN DEPRESSION

YOUR TEEN'S DEPRESSION IS NOT A REFLECTION ON YOU. Get over yourself and get your kid some help. A friend of my 16-year-old took himself to the doctor and got a prescription for an antidepressant. When he brought the prescription home, his parents flipped out. "What if someone finds out?" and "We are *not* bad parents. You are being dramatic." Luckily, after two weeks the parents gave permission for him to fill the prescription. He is much better now, has been accepted into the college of his choice, and plans on staying on the meds until his doctor tells him otherwise.

—*YVONNE C. ELWOOD*
GROTON, CONNECTICUT
16 13

NEVER, EVER UNDERESTIMATE A CHILD'S SADNESS! My oldest is on Zoloft. My youngest talks about her depressed feelings to me, but we did not see the need to put her on meds. I attempted suicide in my early 20s. One of my oldest daughter's friends almost got to that point and we interfered. Her mother was furious at first, but then realized that we did the right thing. The girl was a "cutter" and my oldest daughter called 911 one night after talking to her friend on the phone.

—*ANONYMOUS*
TECUMSEH, MICHIGAN
18 15

MY DAUGHTER HAD A TOUGH TIME when she was a teenager. She was down and she was trying to find herself. I sent her to psychologist: she's doing well and she lives in New York now. She makes beautiful jewelry and she's studying business. Maybe sometimes the place is not right for someone and she needs a change.

—*B.*
LOS ANGELES, CALIFORNIA

WHEN OUR SON WAS IN EIGHTH GRADE, we were disciplining him for something and he made a point of telling his mother and me that we didn't realize what a good kid we had. When we pressed him, he told us that some of his friends were drinking, others were doing drugs, and some were experimenting with sex. He let us know that he had many opportunities to engage in all of these. Of course, we were shocked when he told us, but we tried to react in a calm manner so he would continue to confide in us. His point was well taken: We'd had no idea how many temptations were out there for eighth graders, and we agreed that he was doing a hell of a job fending for himself on all these very tricky issues.

> —MR. Z.
> EVANSTON, ILLINOIS
> 😊18 😊16

• • • • • • • •

My daughter's favorite time to tell me things is around midnight. It's tough to stay alert, but it's important.

—N.
BROOKLYN,
NEW YORK
🐕17

I WAS THE WORST TEENAGER IMAGINABLE: I was rebellious and always testing. Whenever my parents closed a door, I opened a new one. It's important to not lose teenagers when they go through these tough stages. Keep communication open and make sure they have a safe place to download their troubles. Once you lose them, that's it: They will go other places for advice where you may not want them to go.

> —A.N.P.
> PITTSBURGH, PENNSYLVANIA

• • • • • • • •

I ONCE READ THAT EVERY ADULT once was a teenager, and that's why we hate teenagers so much. Maybe they remind us of those days of self-doubt and raging hormones. Who wants to be reminded of that?

> —DAVID ARENSON
> JERUSALEM, ISRAEL

ONE DAY MY 15-YEAR-OLD had this tearful confession. She said, "I got something to tell you." I'm thinking, "She's doing drugs, she's pregnant." I'm just trying to stay calm. She said, "Remember when I was supposed to go to water polo practice? I skipped it and I went to watch a video instead!" And then she cried. On the outside, I stayed serious: "Wow, that's pretty serious. We're not going to have any consequences right now, but . . ." On the inside, I was laughing hysterically, thinking, "Oh, my God, I have nothing to worry about!"

—*DEB S.*
SAN DIEGO, CALIFORNIA
21 13

• • • • • • • •

REMEMBER HOW YOU WERE AT THAT AGE. Try to understand the things that frustrate them and what they are trying to get away with. I was a poorly behaved teen. I don't see my daughters getting away with anything as bad as I did.

—*D.M.*
IOWA CITY, IOWA
16 13

• • • • • • • •

TALK, TALK, AND TALK. And change the environment. My son had a series of bad events happen to him within a period of a month: Two muggings, a school incident, and a car accident where we were lucky to walk away. He was very angry and having trouble sleeping. We talked together, cried together, and prayed together. I also had him see a therapist to make sure he was OK. We are lucky to have a lot of good friends whom he talked to. And I took him to the Caribbean for a few days to get a change of scenery.

—*F.C.*
FOREST HILLS, NEW YORK
15

Always, *always* repeat back to them what they have said to you before you say anything else. Most of the time they did not say what they meant.

—*ANNE KUBAS*
DANVILLE,
CALIFORNIA
22 18

KEEPING THE LINES OPEN

ACCORDING TO PSYCHOLOGIST LAUREN SOLOTAR of the May
Institute, it is vital that parents touch base with their adolescents.
These are the years they need you most. To facilitate dialogue,
Solotar suggests the following:

- Get to know your teen's best communication times, and avoid
  serious discussion when he or she is tired or irritable.

- Ask open-ended questions on subjects that are of interest, but
  not threatening, to your child.

- Share information about your own adolescence, but use good
  judgment.

- Show concern or express how you feel about an issue. It is
  important for your kids to understand what you are thinking
  and why.

- Carve out time to get to know school personnel, your teenager's
  friends, and other parents.

- Make sure your kids always can get in touch with you.

THERE WAS A YEAR, at least, when my daughter and I simply could not talk to each other. So we would write each other notes or letters in a spiral notebook. I would write something and leave it open in the bathroom and she would write back. And we were both good at communicating that way. I feel as if I learned a lot about her. You don't have time to explain everything when you're shouting at each other.

　　—*FRAN CASPERSON*
　　WICHITA, KANSAS
　　 34

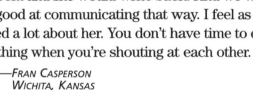

'Never say to your teenager, 'I understand how you feel.' You really don't. Even if your experiences were similar, they are not the same. Things are different than when you were this age. '

　　—*STEVEN A. PARSONS JR.*
　　FT. ASHBY, WEST VIRGINIA
　　 13

BIGGEST MISTAKE PARENTS MAKE with their teenagers? Not communicating with them. And I mean communicating on a regular basis, not just when there are problems. I talked with my teenagers about everything from coloring their hair to the Supreme Court, and lots of funny little things in between. When problems occurred, it didn't feel awkward to talk about them.

　　—*M.S.L.*
　　WAIKOLOA, HAWAII
　　 40 37

SURPRISE! YOUR TEEN WANTS TO HEAR FROM YOU

Seventy percent of teens interviewed said that they were ready to listen to things parents thought they were not ready to hear.

WHEN MY DAUGHTER COMES HOME from school, I always ask how her day was. Ninety-nine times out of a hundred, her response is "fine." Well, I have to tell you, that's just not enough for me. So here's how the rest of the conversation goes: "So, who did you eat lunch with?" And she will tell me. "So, who is your favorite friend today?" And she will tell me. "So, what did you do in your drama class?" And she will tell me. Usually, by the time I get to lunch, I begin to truly get a conversation going. Never accept "fine" as the final word on your child's school day—you'll be missing much of her life.

> —ANONYMOUS
> DENVER, COLORADO
> 🧒 13

• • • • • • • • •

DO NOT STOP SPENDING TIME with your teenager, even though they may act like, or even say they do not want you around (you may have heard a few of these phrases: "I don't want to spend time with you," "You're so embarrassing to be seen in public with," "Please don't talk in front of my friends," "Just drop me off here."). If the truth be known, teenagers are struggling between independence and still wanting to be cared for by their parents, even though your son or daughter would like to think that they do not need you any more. Listening to, spending time with, and knowing your teenager could be the most important thing you do as a parent. Disconnecting with your teenager when they seem to want so badly to disengage with you is a huge mistake.

> —T. HUTCHINS
> BARLING, ARIZONA
> 👦 30 🧒 27 👦 21

The Taming of the Teen: Rules, Discipline, & Enforcement

I t seems to come with puberty—a natural desire to push against authority (you), to test limits (yours), and to find their own limits (this side of death or dismemberment, we hope). While parents agree that rules are good, teenagers just don't see it that way. Ever try telling a six-foot-tall, size-twelve-sneaker-wearing kid to apologize or else go to his room? These parents have tried: read the results below.

ALWAYS KNOW THE NAME OF ONE PARENT who is meaner or stricter than you are. This way, when your child uses the "But everyone is going!" line, you can throw back, "I'll call Melissa's mom. If Melissa can go, you can, too," knowing full well that Melissa's mom would never agree.

> —SUSAN ORLOVSKY
> MANALAPAN, NEW JERSEY
> 29 24

DEVELOP A GOOD COP/ BAD COP ROUTINE WITH YOUR SPOUSE. I WAS THE GOOD COP.

> —ADAIR MORELAND
> KEARNY, NEW JERSEY
> FIVE CHILDREN
> AGES 33-43

I was not afraid to be tough or punish them if I had to. There is nothing like losing privileges to get a teen's attention.

—*ROSEMARY C.*
MONTVILLE,
NEW JERSEY

TREAT YOUR TEENAGER AND HIS FRIENDS as if they are lovable, trustworthy, capable, and admirable—and watch what happens. This doesn't mean they don't need guidance and limits: It simply means that kids need to know you have faith in their goodness. Over the years, I've noticed that most adults treat teens as if they are always on their way to trouble, and I suspect this is why they sometimes make our worst nightmares come true. So act as though you're waiting to catch them doing something right, something noble. You'll be amazed.

—*CINDY LAFERLE*
ROYAL OAK, MICHIGAN
🌸17

• • • • • • • •

WE'RE REALLY TERRIBLE PARENTS. We're completely lax. We've never grounded our children. We don't have any rules they would respect. We have no authority. It started when they were young: I would say, "I'm counting now, don't let me get to 10." And I would get to 10 and nothing would happen. They found out I was bluffing. But our kids are really great kids. I'm not proposing this is how people should raise their kids; we just didn't have any plans.

—*B.S.*
BROOKLYN, NEW YORK
👦22 👧17

• • • • • • • •

TELLING THEM UNTIL YOU'RE BLUE in the face doesn't work. Teenagers see how you conduct yourself. They've got a very critical eye on you. If you're kind, polite, productive, and gregarious, they are, too. If you function in the world with a lot of bad attitude, or by putting on a phony face, they will, too. Or hate you for it.

—*JOHN W.*
LONGMEADOW, MASSACHUSETTS

WHEN MY DAUGHTER WAS RAISING her teenagers, I often expressed to her the importance of not being too strict or too lenient. You have to find the happy medium. You are not your teenager's pal, but you are not their drill sergeant either. If you can consistently find the middle ground when parenting your teenager, you are doing a pretty good job.

> —*M.A.*
> *BARLING, ARIZONA*
> 🐶 *53*

❝I have seen many parents who pressure their kids into a state of permanent anxiety. One parent drove his kids so hard, they lost all the sweetness of their relationship. It became a burden for both. ❞

> —*S.S., COUNSELING OVER 40 YEARS*
> *PASSAIC, NEW JERSEY*
> *FOUR CHILDREN AGES 23-40*

YOU HAVE TO BE CONSISTENT in your discipline. The same infraction has to receive the same punishment time after time. And you have to apply the same punishment across the board with all your kids. No one gets special treatment.

> —*TERRI MASTELL*
> *PETERSBURG, OHIO*
> 👶 *24* 👶 *20*

LYING, WITH PURPOSE

A few weeks ago, my daughter told me she was staying after school to audition for the school play. I thought this sounded suspicious, so, late that afternoon, I drove by the school and saw that her car was gone. When she got home around 5:30 p.m., I asked how the audition went and she said fine.

I told her I'd driven by the school earlier and noticed her car was gone. She explained that she'd moved it to be closer to the auditorium, which still didn't sound right. I sent an e-mail to the drama teacher and found out there were no play tryouts that week. Then, I confronted my daughter and said I knew she'd been lying.

My daughter confessed, saying she'd really been over at a friend's house with no parents around and she knew I wouldn't like that. This explanation still sounded fishy, but she wouldn't say anything else, so we forbade her to drive the car until further notice.

The thing is, prior to this incident, she'd been doing extra chores and collecting lots of allowance, which was unlike her. I was wondering, "Oh, my God! Is she buying drugs? Is she driving to Nebraska to visit her boyfriend?" Then, about two hours later, she came up to me and said, "OK, I'll tell you where I really was. About three weeks ago, I got a speeding ticket and you said that if I got a ticket, you'd take the car away. So I saved up my money and, on the day I said I was auditioning, I drove up to pay the ticket in cash."

The moral? Sometimes you fear the worst, but the truth turns out to be so much better. Even though our daughter lied to us, which isn't cool, we were impressed by her initiative in trying to fix the problem herself, and by how she came clean, so we decided not to take her car away after all.

—M.C.
DENVER, COLORADO
16 13

MY DAUGHTER WANTED TO GO every place all the time. I had to make sure where she was all the time. I was nosy. I asked her, "Where are you going?" And I was the mom that drove; I checked up on her. If she told me she was going to be someplace I would drive by to see if she was there. I never told her that. And I had no problem eavesdropping on my kids. I found out a certain something about my daughter by eavesdropping and it was a good thing, because I stopped her from doing something stupid. I made up an excuse about how I "accidentally" heard her say something to a friend on the phone. Then she told me about it, and we had a talk.

—*T.C.*
SAN DIEGO, CALIFORNIA
 22 👧 20

• • • • • • • •

BE SURE THAT THE TEENAGERS UNDERSTAND the rules and the natural consequences of the rules. For example, your teenager has a chore; say, doing the dishes. He leaves with a friend right after dinner and the dishes are still in the sink. When he comes home, meet him at the door, lead him to the kitchen, and calmly read a book while he does all of the dishes (including a few you added to the mess). He doesn't get to bed until one in the morning, but he has learned that the chore had to be done. Remember, above all, that you are the parent and they are the children. Teenagers may not like that, but they will respect you in the end. If you make adult decisions, they will learn to do the same.

—*DIANE EVANS*
RENTON, WASHINGTON
😊 30 😊 28 😊 26 😊 26 😊 25

> Tell them you're not doing it to be mean or to control them; say, "I'm just doing it because I know best. I've been there."
>
> —*BECKY PAVLIS*
> *KNOXVILLE, TENNESSEE*
> 👧 26

Ordering teenagers around never works. All they'll do is rebel and do the opposite of what you want.

—*ALLAN JAFFE*
PETALUMA,
CALIFORNIA
🌚 21 👶 6

I THINK YOUR TEENS DESERVE TO KNOW what your rules are. Not everyone's rules are the same. But if they know what you expect, they're going to come out just fine. We have certain rules and either they follow the rules or there are consequences. For instance, my son has a car. He's always supposed to call us when he gets to where he's going: If he forgets to call us, then he drops his keys in a drawer at home and he's not allowed to drive the next day. We've done it twice in a year. I don't make threats: There's a rule and there's a consequence.

—*KAREN*
KNOXVILLE, TENNESSEE
🌚 17 🌚 14

* * * * * * * *

MY DAUGHTER HAD A SITUATION COME UP where she was at her friend's house and her friend said, "Let's try this," and they had some liquor. But the next morning she told me about it and said she felt horrible about it. As a parent, you want to tell them that they were wrong for doing that. But you also want them to know it's OK, they're going to make mistakes, and you still love them unconditionally. I don't think teenagers realize, that if they mess up you'll still love them. They don't understand that making mistakes is a way of learning.

—*CINDY STEVENS*
SAN DIEGO, CALIFORNIA
👶 14

* * * * * * * *

NEVER TELL A TEENAGER TO DO SOMETHING you're not already doing yourself. If you tell your teenager to clean his or her room, your own room had better be clean. If you tell your teen not to smoke, you had better not be smoking yourself. Teenagers hate hypocrisy, and do not respond well to the "do what I say, not what I do" philosophy of parenting.

—*RANDY*
OAKDALE, MINNESOTA
👶 13

ONE NIGHT WHEN MY SON WAS ABOUT 16, he had taken the moped to work, about two miles away at a pizza place. After close and cleanup, he didn't come home. It was 3 a.m., and I was still awake and he still wasn't home. I envisioned him in a ditch somewhere. I even drove to the pizza place to look for him. Around 4 or 5 a.m., he finally came home: He'd been at some girlfriend's house or a party. So we talked about him letting us know where he'd be when he was going to come home late. It's important to have that conversation.

—*LORAINE*
BOSTON, MASSACIHUSETTS
38 35

HOW TO GET THEM TO FOLLOW YOUR RULES

Make a set of rules, then categorize them:

- Necessary for family preservation
- Nice to have
- Wish they would

Now, throw out all of the rules in the "Nice" and "Wish" categories, and enforce the "Necessary" ones.

—*DIANE EVANS*
RENTON, WASHINGTON
30 28 26 26 25

ONE TIME MY SON STAYED OUT almost all night. I called the police, the hospitals, and so on. When I finally found him at a friend's house, hanging out with several kids and just talking, I didn't yell at him or ground him. I just sat in the car with him and calmly told him what had been happening while he was missing: Your grandmother has been pacing the floor all night, the police are out looking for you, and so on. He's never done anything like that again.

—*JO E. SHEA*
PARKDALE, OREGON
👦23 👦21 👦19

• • • • • • • •

❝ You have to be like a good football coach. If a kick in the seat is required, then provide it. If all it takes is a stern word to get some action, that's fine, too. ❞

—*PAM SASSER*
WHEELING, WEST VIRGINIA
👦17 👦14 👧10

• • • • • • • •

NEVER DRAW A LINE IN THE SAND with your teenager. If you do, they will push the line every time. It's a subtle game of having rules but not hard and fast ones. Mine broke every rule in the book, but the thing that keeps us balanced is love and patience.

—*IAN WHITEHEAD*
CANYON LAKE, TEXAS
👦25 👧24 👧23 👧23 👦11

ONE MONTH MY DAUGHTER ran up a $250 phone bill talking with a friend in another state. We were so shocked when we saw that bill! My husband and I decided that she would have to pay every cent. With only her allowance and babysitting money, it took her months to pay it off. But my husband and I held our ground and didn't let her quit. She didn't like it, but she paid the whole bill. My daughter's friend's parents, who of course had about the same phone bill, didn't make their daughter repay them. I believe that by making our daughter pay that bill, we helped to teach her that her actions have consequences. I'm sure that's not what her friend learned.

—*CRYSTAL SMITH*
DUBOIS, PENNSYLVANIA
🐵 *19* 🐵 *14*

• • • • • • • • •

IF YOU HARP ON EVERY LITTLE THING, you will lose their attention. Just go for the big stuff! When my girls would snip at each other or make some disparaging sound under their breaths when I was making them do something, I just let it go (no sweating the small stuff). When my middle daughter was supposed to take care of her younger sister and left her at the pizza place by herself after a birthday party, that was a biggie. If there were bad grades or a friend who just didn't seem right or any bizarre behavior that could indicate drugs, those were biggies. Biggies were things that could result in harm or long-lasting damage of some sort.

—*P.M.*
TULSA, OKLAHOMA
🐵 *30* 🐵 *27* 🐵 *25*

Watch out for shifty eyes, shaky bodies, voice fluctuations and a general sense of fear. These are all signs a teenager is lying to you.

—*LAURIE C.*
DENVER,
COLORADO
🐵 *19* 🐵 *14*

I always try to find a win-win and never a win-lose situation. Once you shame or degrade your kid, you erode your influence.

—*Anonymous*
Montclair,
New Jersey

USE THE 20 PERCENT/80 PERCENT RULE to teach teens how to handle problems. Life is 20 percent what happens to you and 80 percent how you react to it. You don't control the 20 percent. But you sure as heck control the 80 percent. I give that advice to teens just before I swear them into military service. One example I give them is about a guy going off to basic training. That guy can't control the fact that he's got this man in a Smokey the Bear hat talking to him in a really loud voice. What he can control is how he reacts to the yelling. That's what drill instructors call "attitude." As long as the guy has the right attitude (i.e. he doesn't react by smarting off), he'll be good to go.

—*Thomas M.W. "Mike" Downs*
Fayetteville, New York
20 16 13 10

• • • • • • • • •

THERE ARE ACTUALLY SOME ADVANTAGES to being a single parent. When there are two parents (unless the parents are *very* together), the teenager can play one off against the other. But all requests, conversations, and permissions, went through me: I ran things. I have control of the one car we have. More important, I had only a few rules when it came time for my son to be out and about—he had to tell me where he was going, write down the address and phone number, and call me and tell me if he was going somewhere else. If he couldn't reach me, he would leave a message on our answering machine.

—*B.C.*
Seattle, Washington
20

I ALWAYS TOLD MY KIDS that no matter how difficult it is and no matter what the crowd is doing, you should always do the right thing. Each and every time you do the right thing, it becomes easier to do the right thing the next time. When my kids were young, before they were even in kindergarten, I had business cards made up that said, "I did it!" I gave them a card whenever they did something good or did something right that I had asked them to do. They saved up their cards and could redeem them for treats. When my kids reached their teens, the rewards changed. They might get an unexpected allowance or a surprise family outing.

—*AL PARISI*
AGOURA HILLS, CALIFORNIA
21   16

BACK ON TRACK

Yelling really doesn't work. As my sons became teenagers, I found myself yelling all the time. I'm five feet eight, and they are all six feet eight, so they tower over me. One day, my sons were playing a horseracing video game. They called me over and said, "Mom, your horse is winning." When I asked them which horse was mine, they said, "The gray one—nag, nag, nag." Soon after that, I took a class on redirecting children's behavior, which is taught all over the country. I learned parenting techniques far better than yelling. I learned how to communicate effectively with my kids. For example, if my sons told a nasty joke in front of me, instead of yelling I'd ask them to stop because those types of jokes make me feel disrespected. This type of communicating is far more effective than engaging in power struggles.

—*SUSIE WALTON*
SAN DIEGO, CALIFORNIA
28   26   24   22

YOU HAVE TO BE UNDERSTANDING and give teenagers good advice, but even if they don't take it, still be there for them. My oldest daughter had some trouble in high school with drugs and boys, but once she got through that period, she realized that she had taken the wrong path. I was there to help her get her GED and I had the chance to see her finish college.

—*JAMES NEWHOUSE*
CIBOLO, TEXAS
42 41 37

Relieve your-
self of the
notion that
your kids will
think you're
cool. They
will not.

—*JAY KLEBANOFF*
NORFOLK, VIRGINIA
13

IN RAISING CHILDREN there has to be a strict "guidelines and consequences" scenario. You have to lay out the rules and the objectives and tell them that these are in place because you love them and you want them to succeed. I used to tell my kids, "As long as you follow the rules and don't abuse our trust and always let us know where you are and do well in school, there is nothing that your mother and I won't do for you. But as soon as you stray off that path and you stop listening and stop doing the things we want you to do, then all of that goes away."

—*BRIAN COY*
SAN DIEGO, CALIFORNIA
22 20

IT'S A PARENT'S JOB to be the heavy sometimes. And honestly, kids can use the help, especially if you have a reputation for being strict. My son, when asked to do something he shouldn't, can say to friends, "You know my mom and dad. They follow me around like stalkers. I'd never get away with it."

—*MARY*
OAKDALE, MINNESOTA
14

THE PROBLEM WITH PARENTS IS that they feel like they are authority machines, and that defeats the purpose of communicating. What teen do you know respects authority? If you're going to lay down the law, you can't expect kids to treat you in a way you want to be treated. You can't expect them to let you into their lives.

—*B.S.*
BROOKLYN, NEW YORK
👶 *22* 👧 *17*

⁶ If your teen is a nightmare, then you have to re-evaluate what you are doing as a parent that might be contributing to that behavior. Teenagers don't just become nightmares without a reason. 🙳

—*MARGARET*
BELLEVUE, WASHINGTON
👧 *27* 👶 *25*

YOU HAVE TO STAY TRUE TO WHAT YOU BELIEVE no matter how much your teenager tries to sandpaper you into changing your mind. I remember last winter it was very icy here and my eldest son wanted to take a drive into the mountains to an ice rink. He thought he'd be safe. I said no and I stuck to my guns. I've learned that with teenagers it's okay to be the mean one and set limits. There are some regrets you just don't want to have.

—*JILL ZIMMERMAN*
ISSAQUAH, WASHINGTON
👶 *19* 👶 *14*

IT'S FOR THEIR OWN GOOD

The first duty of a parent is to be a parent! Because there are so many single-parent families today, I believe that many of these parents suffer from an underlying guilt. This causes them to avoid making their children "buckle down" (as my mother would say) and act in a responsible manner. And, whether they realize it or not, that is probably the single worst thing that they are doing to their kids—not making them shoulder responsibility or pull their own weight in the world.

I was a single mother for quite a few years during my daughter's childhood and I found myself doing the same thing. When I realized what I was doing—even though it made me the bad guy and she whined and complained—I made a special effort to go back and check to see if she was doing what I told her to do, and, if not, I made her do it. It was difficult, it was time-consuming, and I didn't win any popularity contest with her.

But I kept thinking, "What about when she's older and gets a job somewhere? Do I want all of her coworkers to say, 'Oh no! Here she comes, the slacker who never does her part! Now we'll have to work twice as hard to do her job, too!'" And I thought, "No! I want people to love to see my daughter coming. I want them to admire and respect her. And the only way they ever will is if she is a responsible, moral person with good character! And the only way to do that is to keep on top of her activities and make sure she's doing what she's supposed to do!" In one job my daughter had in her late teens, she was voted Employee of the Month three times in nine months. That's my girl!

—*Jean C. Fisher*
Sebastopol, California
🐾 30 🐾 30

WHEN WE GAVE MY DAUGHTER A CAR for high school graduation, we told her that she was the only one who could drive it. But one time she came home and her friend Matt was driving. We sat her down and made it perfectly clear that no one else was to drive because insurance didn't cover it. Two nights later, she left with her friend, and as she was walking out of the house she threw him the keys and he got in the driver's seat. When she came home later, we told her she couldn't use the car for three weeks. She was really, really mad. I think I took the keys to work and hid them there. It was very hard. She thought we were awful, but she didn't do it again.

—*Barbara Ramsey*
Richardson, Texas
👧*32* 🧑*25*

WHAT PARENTS NAG TEENS ABOUT MOST

1. Where they go when they leave the house

2. The TV shows they can watch

3. The movies they watch on the VCR or DVD

4. Time spent with friends

5. What they do online

6. Time spent talking on the phone

7. The kinds of food they eat

8. Time spent watching TV

9. Kinds of music they can listen to

10. Time spent playing video games

ABOUT THAT CURFEW

WE NEVER MADE THE CONSCIOUS DECISION to not give our kids a curfew. They were basically good, happy kids, and they just always seemed to come home when they were ready. It always worked out fine. Of course, we don't know what kind of weird stuff they were doing when we weren't looking.

—*JACK MORRIS*
WALTHAM, MASSACHUSETTS
😊 *42* 🐵 *41* 🐵 *36*

· · · · · · · · ·

ALL THE SAME RULES THAT APPLIED TO OUR SON also applied to our daughter. Especially the curfew. My husband initially wanted to make the curfew earlier for our daughter because "she's a girl." But I insisted that all the kids get treated the same. Equality begins at home!

—*PAGET PERRAULT*
MELBOURNE, AUSTRALIA
😊 *35* 🐵 *30*

· · · · · · · · ·

CURFEWS REALLY NEED TO BE ADJUSTED on a yearly basis. You can't expect your children to be in at the same time when they are in ninth grade as you do when they are seniors. As long as they obey the curfew, extending it slightly each year will show them the increasing confidence and trust that you have in them and it will make them work even harder to be on time.

—*PAULA GRUBBS*
RENFREW, PENNSYLVANIA
🐵 *17* 😊 *15*

· · · · · · · · ·

WE'VE ALWAYS HAD THE RULE: Be home or call by midnight. If he calls because they're watching a movie at someone's house or going out for coffee, fine, but just let us know. He's usually home by midnight.

—*ANONYMOUS*
LITTLETON, COLORADO
😊 *19* 🐵 *13*

THE BEAUTY OF CURFEWS in our area is that they're a law. The perfect way out of a potentially sticky situation is to abide by whatever the law says on weekends. That way, it's not you the kids need to get mad at. You're not the one setting the laws, you're just enforcing them.

—*ROBYN MURAMOTO*
CENTENNIAL, COLORADO
👶 *15* 👶 *13*

• • • • • • • • •

I DEVISED A SYSTEM TO REST BETTER ON WEEKEND NIGHTS when my kids would be out. I would leave three lights in the house on, and the third one was right next to my bed. The last teenager returning had to turn off that light. Nobody wanted to do it, because I would usually wake up, so it helped them make it home on time.

—*ANONYMOUS*
RAYMORE, MISSOURI
👶 *61* 👶 *58*

• • • • • • • • •

WHEN MY SONS WERE OLD ENOUGH TO DRIVE, I started to impose curfews on them. Of course, they challenged me. Why suddenly did they have curfews? When I explained my true fear—that statistics show the highest concentration of drunk drivers are on the road after midnight—they understood.

—*SUSIE WALTON*
SAN DIEGO, CALIFORNIA
👶 *28* 👶 *26* 👶 *24* 👶 *22*

• • • • • • • • •

IF THEY COULD NOT MAKE THEIR CURFEW, they had to call. Always. If they had a good reason, there was no problem. But they had to call us. My son still calls if he's going to be late—and he's 35 years old!

—*ANONYMOUS*
BROOKLYN, NEW YORK
👶 *30* 👶 *28*

WHEN MY SON WAS CONSISTENTLY LATE, I found that restricting him one hour for every five minutes of lateness was very effective. He learned that being on time is important, as well as how to calculate complicated 5:1 ratios.

—*SHELLEY*
TAMPA, FLORIDA
😊 *17* 👧 *12*

• • • • • • • •

" "My biggest weapon was my husband, who would give the girls what they called 'The Look.' I think The Look did more than any punishment. We still laugh about it today. " "

—*SUE LYNN*
FORT LAUDERDALE, FLORIDA
👧 *50* 👧 *46* 👧 *45*

• • • • • • • •

PRESENT A UNITED FRONT. Very early in life, kids learn the "divide and conquer" technique—if one parent doesn't let you do what you want, go ask the other one. This is tough when kids are young, but believe me, they get even better at it when they're teenagers. Now more than ever, my husband and I present a united front to our teens. We compare notes often, and our kids know they cannot get away with playing us against each other. We back each other up—if my husband tells the kids something I support him one hundred percent.

—*CRYSTAL SMITH*
DUBOIS, PENNSYLVANIA
👧 *19* 😊 *14*

MY OLDER DAUGHTER KNEW EVERYTHING about my past. A young teenager doesn't know how to see these things in perspective. We got to a point where every time I'd reprimand her, she'd say, "You have no right to talk." And the do-as-I-say-not-as-I-did thing doesn't work. I don't think you have to lie to your kids, just shield them a little. Don't romanticize your own misguided youth, don't try to make them think you're cool by telling them more than they need to know. My younger daughter doesn't know that stuff about me, and we're having less trouble with her.

—*J.G.*
CHAPEL HILL, NORTH CAROLINA
17 13

Pretend to believe everything and believe nothing.

—*G.T.*
PITTSBURGH, PENNSYLVANIA

• • • • • • • •

WE'RE NOT BIG BELIEVERS IN SETTING RULES about curfews, grades or dating—we'd rather have our son learn responsibility on his own. This usually works really well because he's actually harder on himself than we would've been. For example, recently, he stayed at a friend's house watching hockey until 11:30 on a school night. The next morning, he was completely exhausted. So, instead of lecturing, we sat down and talked about why staying out that late wasn't a good idea. His response? "Yeah, it's no fun being tired at school. I really can't do that again!"

—*KARI GOERKE*
CENTENNIAL, COLORADO
14 11

• • • • • • • •

MY KIDS KNOW THEY HAVE NO PRIVACY in the house. That's a rule. I can and do go through everything. It's my house and they need to know they have no place to hide stuff—period.

—*LEE*
PASSAIC, NEW JERSEY

SLAM THE DOOR ON DOOR SLAMMING

WHEN OUR CHILDREN TURNED 13, we gave them three slips of paper, each with a number written on it (1, 2, 3). Each time something happened to their doors (hard slamming meant a hinge had to be tightened or a door reattached) they had to turn in a slip of paper. If something happened to the door and the teen had already spent her three chances, her door would be removed and her worst nightmare realized—absolutely no privacy or personal space. It worked like a charm!

> —*M.L.M.*
> *SPRINGFIELD, ILLINOIS*
> *21* *19* *16* *14*

* * * * * * * * *

I NEVER ALLOWED MY TEENAGERS TO SLAM DOORS. They knew if they slammed it, their bedroom door was coming off the hinges for a week.

> —*LARRY NEEDY*
> *LOUISVILLE, KENTUCKY*
> *36* *31* *29* *28*

* * * * * * * *

SHE ALWAYS SLAMMED THE DOOR right after I'd say, "And don't slam the door!" So I stopped saying it.

> —*N.*
> *BROOKLYN, NEW YORK*
> *17*

MAKE SURE WHEN YOU ARE PUNISHING your teen that you pick a punishment that will mean something to them. It takes some thought. When my first son was a high school junior, he and a couple of guys went out and bought some beer and went over to the high school and sat in the parking lot and drank. They went into a school dance, and the principal smelled the beer. They got into trouble, including in-school suspension. It was right before he was old enough to get his driver's license. We decided not to let him get one. That would be a big deal to most teens, but we found out later that he didn't care because he had a girlfriend who was a little older and she could drive.

—JANET VALLONE
WAYMART, PENNSYLVANIA
👶34 👶31 👶27

Don't ground them for a month; you won't stick to it. When they're grounded, you're grounded, too.

—KATE
ALFORD,
MASSACHUSETTS

• • • • • • • •

WHENEVER WE HAD MAJOR CONFLICTS when the kids were little, we'd give them timeouts. We used it as a way to isolate the children so that they could stop and think about what was going on. But I found that as the kids got older and I became a single parent, it worked best when *I* took a timeout. If things got really hot and there was lots of yelling and the situation was getting out of hand, *I* would go to *my* room. I would tell the kids, "Leave me alone until I can deal with this." It would help all of us cool down and think about things, and the kids didn't feel that I was trying to control them.

—K.M. CARTER
DES MOINES, IOWA
👶21 👶19

If you figure out what to do with a defiant kid, let me know. I found the only solution was to wait it out.

—*Anonymous*
Montclair,
New Jersey

I accidentally found out my daughter was skipping school. I was emptying the wastepaper basket in her room, and I found all these notes supposedly written by me excusing her from class. She didn't get into trouble often, but I wanted her to know this was serious. You have to make a stand about things that are important to you. So I got in the car and drove over to an entertainment complex, a game place, where she and the rest of the family were having fun. I made her come home, and she was grounded for a long time. I think she got the message.

—*Midge Ramsey*
Averill Park, New York
42 37

• • • • • • • • •

My daughter and her friend snuck out of our house late one night and I caught them. We lived across the street from the golf course and they apparently wanted to go walking. But I heard her go downstairs. I waited until they were gone and I locked all the doors. Then I went to the garage door and disconnected the keypad to get in. When they came back an hour and a half later, they couldn't get in the house. I walked outside by the front door, snuck around to the garage, and said, "What are you girls doing?" It scared them to death.

—*Pat Williams*
Atlanta, Georgia
21 19

Earning Their Stripes: On Independence & Responsibility

J ust when you thought your teen couldn't be more irresponsible, here he is, demanding even more responsibility and independence! (And he won't stop, not until he has all the responsibility and independence he can take.) For now, you have to learn to let go, help him take his first steps toward adulthood, and (gasp!) hand him the keys to your car.

WORKING IS THE BEST WAY to keep your teens out of trouble. Our girls worked during their high school years at the local supermarket and it limited outside activities enough to curb our worries. Too much free time can be a problem.

—*HARRY RAMSEY*
VENICE, FLORIDA
🐶 42 🐶 37

WHEN MY KIDS WERE TEENAGERS, I TOLD THEM, "HURRY UP AND MOVE OUT BEFORE IT'S TOO LATE."

—*ANONYMOUS*
LONG VALLEY, NEW JERSEY
🐶 32 🐟 23

It's downright scary to face the fact that there is no way to be with them every second to be sure of their safety without taking back all the freedom and rights they have earned.

—*Rita Porter*
Springfield,
Missouri
14

By the time teenagers get to be about 16 you should stop treating them like kids and start treating them like adults. This can be hard for parents who don't want to admit that their little babies are growing up. But it's the only way to get them ready for the real world that they will be entering soon.

> —*Eileen*
> *Pittsburgh, Pennsylvania*

• • • • • • • •

It's a teenager's nature to want to explore and investigate and try things that in a perfect world we would keep them away from. It's not that they are disrespectful or don't trust us as parents, but it's almost an instinct for kids that age to want to try new things.

> —*Tanya West*
> *Frostburg, Maryland*
> *13*

• • • • • • • •

Adolescence is nature's way of transitioning from childhood to adulthood. Testing the boundaries of independence is an inevitable part of that development.

> —*Ruth Drescher*
> *Pittsburgh, Pennsylvania*
> *44 42 40*

• • • • • • • •

I believe if you give a person something, they don't appreciate it as much as when they put their own blood, sweat, and tears into earning it. We buy my son's clothes for him and he doesn't treat them well. But don't walk past his car: Don't even lean up against it. He has $3,000 invested in it!

> —*Gary Collins*
> *Tampa, Florida*
> *17*

IT SEEMS TO ME THAT TEENAGERS TODAY have a need to grow up too fast. What happened? Teenage years should be spent having fun and should not be complicated. Why hurry the time you have to grow as a person?

—*S.F.*
BUFFALO GROVE, ILLINOIS
22 20

. . . .

❛You have to give as much attention to your teenagers as you did when they were babies. Just because they are old enough to drive doesn't mean they don't need you. The fact that they don't ask for it, doesn't mean they don't want you to be part of their life. ❞

—*BOB SCHULTZ*
HOPEWELL TOWNSHIP, PENNSYLVANIA

. . . .

WE RAISED OUR CHILDREN to be very strong-willed and independent. Then when they became teenagers, we paid for it. They never quite got it that they were supposed to be opinionated with everyone but us!

—*ANONYMOUS*
DES MOINES, IOWA

DRIVING YOU CRAZY

FROM THE DAY MY KIDS TURN 15 to the moment they get their driving permits, I take them to the graveyard to practice driving every day. It's important to get as much behind-the-wheel experience as possible before going out on real roads, and the graveyard is an excellent place to practice; it has streets, stop signs and very little traffic. Plus, I always joke they can't kill anybody, since everybody is already dead!

—*CHERI HURD*
LITTLETON, COLORADO
👩26 👦23 👩21 👦14

• • • • • • • •

THE GOOD THING ABOUT THE KIDS DRIVING stick-shift cars is that they have to pay attention to driving, so they're less apt to yak on the phone.

—*WILLIAM SMITH*
SAN FRANCISCO, CALIFORNIA
👩23 👩21 👦16

• • • • • • • •

DRIVE WITH YOUR TEENAGER FOR THE FIRST 5,000 MILES before they get their license. Someone told my husband that teenagers have more accidents in this period than at any other time. Clinging to our lives, my husband and I did this with both of our daughters. We drove on highways, dark alleys, and back roads so they would be prepared for any kind of situation.

—*S.F.*
SAN ANTONIO, TEXAS
👩20 👩16

• • • • • • • •

I DON'T THINK ANY JOB AS PARENT requires as much patience as does teaching kids how to drive. Whatever meditation techniques you've picked up over the years to calm yourself, you are going to need to use them during this. I nearly wore out the rug on the passenger's side floor from hitting the brake that wasn't there.

—*E.P.*
CRANBERRY TOWNSHIP, PENNSYLVANIA
👦27 👩24

I TRIED MY BEST TO TEACH MY SON everything I could about his car, which is a 1997 Ford Ranger stick. I went over maintenance and other mechanical things in great detail until I was confident he knew how to operate that vehicle inside and out. Unfortunately, I didn't do as good a job as I'd thought: The first night my son had his license, a policeman pulled him over as he was getting on the highway. Startled, my son looked up at the officer and squeaked, "I wasn't speeding, was I?" The officer shook his head and smiled, then reached in and clicked his headlights on. In my haste to educate my son about cars, I forgot to mention the simplest thing of all!

—*MARK SCOTT*
SAFFORD, ARIZONA
🙂 *16* 🙂 *13*

• • • • • • • •

SEND THEM TO DRIVING SCHOOL, then take a Xanax and get in the car.

—*ANONYMOUS*
CHICAGO, ILLINOIS
👧 *24* 👧 *20* 🙂 *19* 🙂 *17* 👧 *15*

• • • • • • • •

WHEN I WAS TEACHING MY OLDEST HOW TO DRIVE, I took her to the church parking lot. It was the perfect place because she could practice and I could pray at the same time.

—*L.E.*
POMONA, CALIFORNIA
👧 *17* 👧 *12*

• • • • • • • •

NOTHING GIVES A PARENT MORE SLEEPLESS NIGHTS than those times your teenager is out with the car late at night. Nobody is getting any sleep until you hear that car in the driveway. I remember when my kids were babies and I thought I had it tough. A friend of mine told me to wait until they started driving, and now I know why.

—*PATTY KRAMER*
PITTSBURGH, PENNSYLVANIA
👧 *33* 👧 *31*

They're not always going to do what you want them to do. You just have to plant the right seeds. And hope.

—*CINDY STEVENS*
SAN DIEGO,
CALIFORNIA
14

YEARS AGO, I LET MY HIGH-SCHOOL-AGE daughter arrange a family trip for us. She did the research and found us a condo at Lake Tahoe. We had skied there a bit as a family, and she had friends who skied there, so she took the initiative to find a place for us. She showed me all of the paperwork that I was to sign off on, and even arranged a family dinner with our friends and neighbors who were up skiing that week. My wife and I had been thinking it would have been fun to go to Hawaii, but once my girls spoke up and said they'd prefer a ski trip, I stepped back. It was empowering for my daughter.

—*DAVID C.*
SAN FRANCISCO, CALIFORNIA
31 29

• • • • • • • •

MY SON LEARNED A VALUABLE LESSON in trust just this past year. He and a friend were shopping at the mall. When they came out and started walking to their car a guy approached them and said he would give them free tickets to a concert if they would drive him to his car, which was broken down at a nearby gas station. They said OK. So this guy started talking to them and told them how he worked in the entertainment industry. He convinced them he could get them backstage passes to all the concerts in the city for the next year for a small fee, but he needed the money up front. They paid, and he asked them to take him home so he could get the passes. What came next was no surprise to me. He got out and never came back. My son said they sat there for like 20 minutes before they realized what had happened. He said he felt so stupid, but I told him it was a cheap lesson and he was lucky he didn't get hurt.

—*BILL NANCIK*
CANFIELD, OHIO
17

IT'S IMPORTANT THAT TEENS FEEL that they have a say in their lives. Giving them ultimatums, like "You will not ____," and "Right now, do ____," isn't a good idea. Teens are supposed to be growing up and becoming independent: it's counterproductive to not give them choices in their lives. Instead, empower them to make the right choices, and use options that you know you can live with.

—*LENI KASS*
CHICAGO, ILLINOIS
15

. . . .

TEACH KIDS THE VALUE OF WORK and money at an early age. My son worked this past summer for a family friend; raking leaves, picking vegetables, and watering her plants. He worked two to three times a week for four hours at a stretch, and she paid him for his work. My son was very proud of himself, and he saved enough money for a gas-powered, remote-controlled car that he really wanted.

—*DEB UHLER*
HELLERTOWN, PENNSYLVANIA
14 10

. . . .

ONE THING TO MAKE SURE TO DO: Teach your teenager how to handle money. When my daughter turned 16, I got her a checking account because I thought she needed to learn about checks and credit cards. Where we live, the bank won't give a 16-year-old a checking account, so it's a joint account between the two of us. Of course, one of the first things our daughter did was bounce a few checks—and she didn't want to hear anything about how to figure your balance. I wish I'd taught her all this a little earlier.

—*JANE*
BROOKLYN, NEW YORK
16 2

TEEN TOPIC

Twenty percent of 16-year-old drivers will be involved in a crash at some point during their first year of driving. The accident rate is the highest during the first month.

MY SON RECENTLY STARTED delivering the daily paper here in town. Being a paperboy is the perfect first job for a kid. Essentially they are working for themselves. They are in charge of delivering the product and collecting payment for it. There is so much to be learned about money, responsibility, and meeting deadlines: Every kid should do it. My son loves having his own spending money. What he doesn't love is getting up at five o'clock to do it.

—*ARTHUR ZIMMERMAN*
YOUNGSTOWN, OHIO
13

" Teach your teenagers money management skills and how to save money. Allow them to earn their allowance, and help them to understand the value of money. "

—*BILL W.*
SEATTLE, WASHINGTON
26 23

EVERY TEENAGER SHOULD GO off for a summer, or part of a summer, and be a camp counselor or counselor-in-training. It teaches them to be responsible for themselves as well as for others. It lets them earn a little money, perhaps. And it is loads of fun.

—*MARTY*
CHICAGO, ILLINOIS
17 15

MY RULE IS: If you're going to be late, call me. If you call and say, "I slipped up and I'm going to be 15 minutes late," then it's OK. It doesn't count.

—*GARY COLLINS*
TAMPA, FLORIDA
17

• • • • • • • •

WE OPENED CHECKING ACCOUNTS for our kids when each one was 13. This wasn't easy: banks won't let you do that in California. But our credit union would. Both kids are now financially responsible. My daughter has never bounced a check. And my son enjoys using his debit card and is very good at keeping track of his money— he even figured out how to transfer funds from one of his accounts to the other on the Internet: Now, *that's* an important life skill. The more responsibility you allow your children to take on for themselves, the better off they are, the more wisdom they can develop, and the better decisions they can learn to make.

—*G.B.*
LOS ANGELES, CALIFORNIA
21 14

• • • • • • • •

OUR KIDS TAKE TURNS DOING CHORES. One week, our son does the dishes every night, washing them by hand, and our daughter is responsible for feeding our dog and two turtles and cleaning up the dog poop. The next week they switch. The kids don't get an allowance for these chores; they're just expected to do them. Sometimes in the summer if they do a larger task, such as mow the lawn, they'll earn some money. But otherwise, they don't get an allowance. If they truly need something, we buy it for them.

—*BARB DANYLUK*
BETHLEHEM, PENNSYLVANIA
15 12

Allow them some decision-making.

—*L.D.*
DARLINGTON, MARYLAND
33 31

THE KEYS TO SANITY

DON'T LET YOUR KIDS LEARN HOW TO DRIVE on your car. Buy them an old beater so that it doesn't matter if they scrape it on a light pole or wear out the brakes. It will alleviate some of your stress if you don't have to worry about your child and your $30,000 SUV at the same time.

> —*ANONYMOUS*
> *PITTSBURGH, PENNSYLVANIA*
> 16

AFTER A BASEBALL GAME MY SON ASKED if he could drive home, and I said yes. The drive home was very uneventful; however, as he pulled into our two-car garage, very carefully easing the car into its appointed slot, it appeared he was not stopping. When it was suggested that he use the brake he hit the accelerator instead—and continued to go right through the garage wall. At the time, my daughter and her boyfriend were inside the house, and they thought the house was falling down.

> —*NOLA SMITH*
> *TAMPA, FLORIDA*
> 41 36

ONE TIME MY SON HAD TO HAUL TRASH TO THE DUMP. We were living in the mountains at the time, it was snowing, and we had icy roads. I checked the weather report, and the main roads were fine. But he decided to go to the next town first to get a coffee at Starbucks. He picked the iciest, shadiest road to get down there and spun out on the ice. If it weren't for an elm tree, he might have veered into a ditch and flipped over. The car was totaled. When I got there, he was shaking. Of course, we had a discussion about doing exactly what I tell him. If it hadn't been for that tree, he'd be dead now as a result of poor decision-making. When I let him go, I had one of those twinges: Maybe I shouldn't have let him go. The problem with those things is, you never know what they mean until it's too late.

> —*DAN O'TOOLE*

MAKE TEENS PAY THEIR OWN DEBTS, no matter what the cost. They will value money, hard work and possessions that much more. Our teenage daughter got a ticket for speeding. We made her pay for the tickets out of her own summer job earnings and we showed her how the insurance premiums skyrocketed as a result of her lead foot. She quickly decided it was better to drive the speed limit than to incur expenses she didn't want.

>—*ANN HAALAND*
>*HIGHLAND, NEW YORK*
>*23 20*

. . . .

MY FRIEND'S SON WENT AWAY TO COLLEGE. One day, his parents received a speeding ticket in the mail that had been taken by one of those photo radar cameras near campus. It was sent to the parents because this kid's home address was listed on his driver's license. Instead of calling him up and ragging on him, his parents silently paid the fine. At Christmas, they put the ticket, with "Paid" written across it, in his stocking. His brother, meanwhile, got money.

>—*KATHY MCCLINTIC*
>*CENTENNIAL, COLORADO*
>*27 23*

. . . .

ON THE FIRST DAY OF MY YOUNGEST SON'S SOPHOMORE YEAR in high school, I let him drive to school. I was sitting in the front passenger seat because he only had his permit. He drove through an intersection and, because he wasn't paying attention, didn't see that the car in front of him was braking. He hit that car, demolishing it, and caused a chain reaction of four other vehicles, right in front of the school! Luckily, nobody was hurt, but regardless, I don't think you should let your kids drive to school on the first day.

>—*L.A.*
>*CLEVELAND, OHIO*
>*23 21*

I used to drive
by to check
on my teens
without them
knowing, or
I'd call to
check on
where they
were. It was
the best way
to monitor
them and
avoid a fight.

—*B.L.*
CHICAGO, ILLINOIS
23 *20*

OUR GIRLS GET $20 A MONTH for allowance; however, they only get to keep half. The other half goes into a savings account they manage. This money can be used later for big-ticket items, like a cell phone or a car. We allow them to do whatever they want with the other half of their allowance, free and clear. They also get to choose how to spend their birthday money and anything they earn for doing odd jobs. We've had this system for two years, and both girls have more than $300 in their accounts. If you do the math, this means they have occasionally chosen to put away more than the $10 per month we require. Obviously, they are learning to appreciate the value of saving.

—*ROB MCHARGUE*
SAN ANTONIO, TEXAS
12 *11*

• • • • • • • •

MY 16-YEAR-OLD DAUGHTER WASN'T HAPPY at home because she thought her mother and I were too restrictive. She had a girlfriend who'd had a truly awful home life and had asked for and been granted emancipation. This young woman lived on her own and worked and went to school, and my daughter decided she wanted to do that. My wife was opposed to it, but I told my daughter that if she could make it work it was OK. She spent the summer living with her girlfriend, but when the school year started, she wanted to come back home. She'd found that living on her own was more work than she'd anticipated and home life wasn't so bad after all. If I'd said no to my daughter when she asked to move out, she probably would have run away from home and done it anyway. By allowing her to try some-thing for herself, her mother and I were able to maintain a good relationship with her.

—*M.E.W.*
GLADSTONE, OREGON
45 *41*

THE MULTIPLEX DILEMMA

Recently, my daughter went to a movie with friends. She said the movie they were going to see was PG-13, which is fine. However, for whatever reason, they couldn't get into that movie, so they decided to see something R-rated instead (another parent bought the tickets). My daughter knew this wasn't allowed, but instead of standing up to her friends, she kept quiet and saw it anyway.

When I found out about this, I was extremely upset. From that point on, I started getting really suspicious of her, cross-examining her left and right every time she went to the mall or did anything. Then, I heard these teens talking at a parent forum at the high school. They kept saying stuff like, "Don't assume when your teen wants to hang out with friends that it's because she wants to do drugs." It hit me that I was being overly vigilant and I needed to back off and be a little more trusting. Overall, my daughter is pretty responsible person who knows right from wrong. She may mess up occasionally, but she just wanted to have some fun with her friends.

—*ANONYMOUS*
CLEVELAND, OHIO
14 11

I THINK IT'S GOOD TO GIVE TEENS an allowance to teach them to handle money. My daughters both got allowances from an early age, and they continued to get allowances into their teen years. However, they also did a lot of chores around the house, such as cleaning, laundry, taking care of the pets, and more. They took turns washing the dishes every night, and I dried them.

—*ANONYMOUS*
ALLENTOWN, PENNSYLVANIA
33 31

• • • • • • • •

I'd always let my son know when an adult friend would mention seeing him in the neighborhood. I figured he should be aware that even if I was not around, others who knew him might be watching.

—*P.W.*
BROOKLYN,
NEW YORK
19

I ALLOWED MY DAUGHTERS to be independent as much as possible and to learn how to accept responsibility for their actions. Sometimes that meant taking a "tough love" position. For example, when my daughter decided that she would not go to college, I made her move out of the house, find a job, and support herself. Within a year, she decided that she wanted to go to college, after all. Now, she's a successful engineer. It was hard not to give her money when she needed it, but she had to accept responsibility for her decisions. And, yes, I realize that it could have backfired!

—*VIRGINIA T.*
CHICAGO, ILLINOIS
34 34 29 26

• • • • • • • •

THEY'VE GOT TO DISAGREE WITH YOU on the way you do things or they'll never figure out how to do it themselves. It's a difficult time when you're not making all their decisions for them anymore. You have to let them make mistakes, which is painful. It's probably the hardest part of raising a teenager.

—*JANE*
BROOKLYN, NEW YORK
16 2

I SEE PARENTS AS MENTORS for their teens. Teens should be making their own decisions and furnishing their own motivation. If they don't, they will truly be lost by the time they move out of the house and go off to college or to a job in the real world.

—*G.B.*
LOS ANGELES, CALIFORNIA
 *21* *14*

. . . .

6 Give your teen enough slack that he can become his own person, but keep close enough tabs on him that he doesn't become too influenced by others. It's a fine line to walk, but if you do it well, you'll raise a good person. **99**

—*TILLY*
CHAMPAIGN, ILLINOIS
15

. . . .

AS THE TIME APPROACHES, when my daughter will be deciding on a college and career path, I am careful to let her make her own decisions and not to judge her career choices as right or wrong. Right now she wants to be a lawyer, and I know that might change. I tell her to do what she loves, to find her passion. If you do what you love, success and fulfillment will follow.

—*LENI KASS*
CHICAGO, ILLINOIS
15

TEEN TOPIC

In a recent poll, 33 percent of teens said they would act unethically to make money or to get ahead, if no one else would find out.

WHEN YOU FORCE A CHILD to do something, he will have one of two responses: either he will accept it and knuckle under and lose part of himself, or he will rebel big-time. As a teen, my daughter wanted to go to these all-night arts performances without an adult. I knew if I prevented her she would just sneak around. Instead, I made my feelings plain but left the decision up to her. She went a few times but I was able to trust my child's judgment.

　　—S.B.
　　　KERALA, INDIA
　　　👧26

• • • • • • • •

THEY ARE GAINING INDEPENDENCE at this age. Let them make mistakes: That's one of the biggest learning tools. If it's something really important to you, you have to step in: You do have to stick by your values. But if it's something like a term paper that's due, and they are running late, don't say anything. It's better for them to not get the grade they want or to have to stay up late two nights in a row to finish the paper. It's important to let go so they can figure things out for themselves.

　　—SUETTA GRIFFITH
　　　FISHERSVILLE, VIRGINIA
　　　👧33 👦31

• • • • • • • •

IT IS A SURE SIGN THAT YOUR TEEN is *not* maturing when he gets into two accidents, receives two tickets, and is escorted home by a police helicopter for erratic driving, all within six months. Do not be afraid to revoke his license. Do not wait for a court to do it. Do not assume that 16 is the perfect driving age for all teens.

　　—SHELLEY
　　　TAMPA, FLORIDA
　　　👦17 👧12

NEVER TREAT A TEENAGER LIKE AN ADULT! I know that sounds strange and, perhaps, mean. But teenagers are not able to handle many adult issues. When I was going through my divorce, our children were teenagers. While we discussed the basic information about the divorce and how it would affect our family, we did not discuss the reasons for the divorce, which were quite complicated even for an adult. Many people feel that teenagers are just like adults, but it's not true. They are not emotionally or mentally mature enough to handle certain adult issues, no matter how mature they might seem. I'm glad that the one thing my ex-husband and I agreed on was that our teenagers had to be protected from the messiness and sadness of our divorce.

—*INGELA KOPONEN*
SWEDEN
35 33

TEEN TOPIC

The number one car choice for teenagers is the Honda Civic.

• • • • • • • •

WHEN OUR DAUGHTER WAS 17 she suddenly informed us that she was quitting high school and moving with her girlfriend to New York City. I was terrified. Luckily, instead of trying to stop her or yelling and screaming, I asked if she would sit down with us and write down the advantages and disadvantages of moving. We had her make a list of all the things she would need before she moved and what to do once she got there. We made sure she was as emotionally and financially prepared as possible. She did, indeed, move to New York City, but not as soon as she'd originally planned and after a lot more thought about it ahead of time. We were still petrified. She ended up having a wonderful year and returned safe and sound, after learning about living on her own.

—*A.B.*
CHICAGO, ILLINOIS
27 23 23 21 10

I LEARNED IT'S NOT A GOOD IDEA to have more than a glass of wine, if that, when your kids are out on a weekend night. You never know when you will get a call. Three of my four children were in car accidents when they were teenagers. I've gotten three calls from the hospital; two of them were about my son.

—*L.M.*
FALMOUTH, MAINE
👦35 👧35 👦29 👧23

• • • • • • • •

❝Trust them. Most of the time, my teens did the right thing when I gave them freedom. It's when I tried to box them in that they wanted to break out.❞

—*JULIE CAMPBELL*
NEW YORK, NEW YORK
👦14 👧10

• • • • • • • •

A CAR IS ONE OF THE WORST THINGS you can give a kid. There are so many implications. If you're rich, you're giving your kid a false sense of empowerment. Accidents and speeding tickets cause insurance rates to rise. And, if an 18-year-old gets a DUI, who do you think is going to pay the $10,000 fine? Believe me, if you can withstand the peer pressure from other parents, you're much better off not buying your kids a car.

—*S. BILBY*
ARVADA, COLORADO
👦34 👦31 👧29

IT WAS SUGGESTED ON THE RADIO that kids' weekly allowance equal their ages, with the stipulation they must put half into a savings account. My husband and I liked this suggestion, so we agreed to follow it, although we added a stipulation of our own: Each week, we gave out the money in different denominations. Some weeks, it would be in all dollars, other weeks in all quarters or dimes. We'd occasionally shortchange them on purpose to make certain they were keeping track. This was our way of teaching them the value of money, and it turned out to be a godsend. Today, both of our kids have huge savings accounts, and they are very financially responsible.

—*P.O.*
NEW BRUNSWICK, NEW JERSEY
18 15

You have to give teenagers responsibilities and treat them like capable human beings. It gives them something to live up to.

—*NICK DURHAM, NORTH CAROLINA*
20

• • • • • • • •

MY TEENAGE SON WANTED TO MOVE OUT while still in high school. My husband and I forbade him from moving out for months. Finally we decided that if he wanted to move out and find his own apartment, we would allow it. But he would never be allowed to move back home. We made that clear to him. He moved out and several times wanted to move back home again: We refused. He was forced to get a job and support himself. He faltered a little but, eventually, he found a job and an apartment. Luckily, he finished school. Today, he remembers that as being the time when he finally grew up. He went to college and continued to support himself. He's still doing very well today. It was a risky move, but it did force him to grow up.

—*NAN B.*
WILLIAMSBURG, VIRGINIA
34

DON'T GIVE THEM THE KEYS TO THE CAR until they are at least 18. I don't care if the law does permit them to drive at 16. There is really nowhere that a child of that age needs to go in a car by themselves. But that means as a parent you have to make the commitment to drive them places.

—*WILLIAM GREEN*
FROSTBURG, MARYLAND
22

• • • • • • • •

MY YOUNGEST WAS IN A ROCK BAND: That was interesting. My husband and I wanted to be supportive so we went to one of his gigs at this place called The Cave. Apparently, my son's band had written songs that had a lot of profanity in them. So he told his band. "Don't do that one. My parents are in the audience." Well, they came out and played this one song. The entire song consisted of the F-word, in different tempos. Later, the singer came out with a black eye—my son beat the crap out of him! My son felt it was his place to not offend me. He cared about what his mother thought.

—*CAREN MASEM*
GREENSBORO, NORTH CAROLINA
33 28

• • • • • • • •

WE'VE CONVINCED MY DAUGHTER that we trust her judgment but are concerned for her physical safety when she goes out. She's responded by being very good about letting us know where she is and who she's with. As far as what she's doing… well, that's where her judgment is put to the test.

—*N.*
BROOKLYN, NEW YORK
17

Wild at Heart: Rebelling Through Personal Appearance

When they were born, they were perfect: that smooth skin, that soft hair, those unpierced ears. Now that they're teens, they're beginning to look different—and Mother Nature isn't doing all the alterations. Whether your teen has dyed hair, or tattoos, or pierced body parts, or a penchant for wearing revealing clothes, your kid is still in there somewhere. Here's how to get through this stage without losing your own hair.

WHEN YOUR DAUGHTER COMES HOME with purple hair, give her a big hug and tell her you love her. Ditto when she brings home her first puppy.

—*GEORGINA*
ATLANTA, GEORGIA
35

IT'S JUST HAIR. IT WILL GROW OUT.

—*BECKY WAHKINNEY, PH.D.*
NORMAN, OKLAHOMA
20

If my son
wants a body
piercing, I'll
offer to do it
myself for half
the cost.

—*Denise L.*
Chicago, Illinois
13

LET THEM BE THEMSELVES. But draw the line when you think things have gone too far. Our daughter is constantly begging for piercings, and I have decided that I don't have a problem with her putting a few holes in her ears—but absolutely no tongues, noses or other body parts allowed!

—*Larry Neth*
Highlands Ranch, Colorado
16   9

• • • • • • • •

A TEEN'S APPEARANCE is one of those areas where parents should back off a little and not be so uptight with their kids. You have to let them experiment, express themselves, and get a sense of who they are. As long as they practice good hygiene I don't think it's a big deal if the hair gets a little long (or real short) or if the jeans are ripped and torn (as long as they're clean). Relax and realize you did things that drove your parents up the wall, and you all survived.

—*Dylan Toomey*
Wheeling, West Virginia
20

• • • • • • • •

WHEN MY DAUGHTER was at Catholic school, the uniform included a white blouse. So, all the girls wore colorful Victoria's Secret bras and unbuttoned their tops very low. When she tried to leave the house like that my husband threw a fit, and she buttoned up. At the time, I worked at the school, in the bookstore. When I saw her in school that day, the buttons were undone; it was the fashion. I didn't say anything to her. You have to give kids a little space; you can't control everything. And they aren't going to be like you are in every respect.

—*Carolyn H. Kane*
Hockesin, Delaware
26   19

DO YOU REMEMBER THE DAYS when going braless was cool? My two girls, when they were 15 and 16, would try to sneak out for high school without a bra. I'd yank them back inside and make them put their bras on. I know that the minute they got to school they took them right off; but you do what you can.

—*BARBARA STEVENS*
GATLINBURG, TENNESSEE
👧47 👧45 😊44

• • • • • • • •

❝I absolutely do not allow my son or daughters to get any tattoos or weird piercings while they're living under my roof. My feeling is that whatever they do in their early years reflects back on me as their parent and guardian. When they turn 18 and move out, whatever they want to do to their own bodies is up to them. ❞

—*ANTHONY MANUEL*
KINDER, LOUISIANA
😊17 👧14 👧11

AFTER SCHOOL ONLY

When my daughter turned 14, I told her it was OK to start experimenting with makeup, but I didn't want her wearing it to school. Everything was fine until one morning when I was driving her to school and I noticed she had put a little makeup on and was no doubt trying to hide it, hoping I wouldn't notice. All the way to school, I kept wondering how to handle this. Should I make a big deal about it because she had disobeyed me? Or should I just let it slide because it wasn't that bad? Right before she got out of the car, I looked over at her and said very clearly, "You did a nice job on your makeup, but I don't want you wearing it to school again."

I thought this reaction was a good compromise. As a parent, it's challenging to find the middle ground between supporting your child's growing up without actually encouraging it. I guess I did a good job in this case because right before getting out of the car, my daughter turned around and smiled at me.

—ANONYMOUS
CLEVELAND, OHIO
14 11

I HAVE TWO GIRLS, ages 13 and 14. So far, they have been very good about what they wear. I told them early on that less is always more when it comes to makeup. They both asked me to teach them, and now they tell me they help their peers with it as well. When it comes to what they wear, I tell them that when they go out, they have a choice of leg or cleavage. It's okay to show one or the other, but never both. Of course, they know how to dress appropriately for any situation, but they also know that a first impression is often based on what you wear. They are in the midst of developing their own style and taste, and I am very proud of them.

> —*SANDRA A.*
> *MARIETTA, GEORGIA*
> 👧 14 👧 13

• • • • • • • •

MY SON'S GIRLFRIEND is very well endowed. She showed up at our house one day wearing a very short skirt and a strappy, low-cut tank top that her boobs were literally hanging out of. I didn't feel comfortable saying so out loud, but I wanted her to cover up. So, when they weren't looking, I turned the air conditioner way up. Within a few minutes, she was eagerly accepting my offer of a sweater!

> —*S.H.*
> *NEW LENOX, ILLINOIS*
> 👦 25 👦 17 👧 15

• • • • • • • •

I HAVE OUTLAWED ANY CLOTHING that is designed to make one look at private parts. No sweatpants with "sexy" written across the butt, or T-shirts with "Feel These" written across the chest.

> —*LENNARD HAYNES, SR.*
> *HOUSTON, TEXAS*
> 👦 17 👦 16 👧 15 👧 14 👧 12

YOU HAVE TO STRIKE A BALANCE between, "The hell you're wearing that outside this house!" and leaving them to develop autonomy all on their own. There's a difference between wearing a trend that's really goofy and looking like a slut. For example, while I might not understand their appeal, baggy pants, fishnet stockings worn over the arms, or flip-flops with jeans are OK. On the other hand, microminiskirts, extremely tight pants, or see-through shirts without bras? Not so much.

—*E.C., WORKS WITH TEENS AGES 15 TO 19*
NEW YORK, NEW YORK

• • • • • • • • •

ON MY PARENTS' 50TH WEDDING ANNIVERSARY, my daughter would *not* get out of car because she was "having a bad hair day." Everyone went to the car and tried to talk her out, but she held her ground. She sat in the car while the photographer we hired took family pictures. We could have made a scene and carried her out, kicking and screaming, but we didn't. She eventually came out.

—*W.S.*
WAYSIDE, NEW JERSEY
😊 *26* 👧 *24* 👧 *18*

• • • • • • • • •

BE PREPARED FOR EACH of your own teens to be completely different. Our teenage son couldn't care less what clothes he wears or how he looks. It can be challenging at holidays and his birthday, because it's hard to buy for him. Our pre-teen daughter is the complete opposite: She has her own style, and she always has to look a certain way.

—*BARB DANYLUK*
BETHLEHEM, PENNSYLVANIA
😊 *15* 👧 *12*

I'd rather have my son color his hair blue than smoke crack.

—*MARK SCOTT*
SAFFORD, ARIZONA
😊 *16* 😊 *13*

WHEN MY DAUGHTER WAS 17, she wanted a tongue piercing. I told her that was fine, as long as she paid for it herself. I figured she was at the age where she was going to do it one way or the other anyway, so why stress out about it? It's just like when girls leave for school wearing a skirt that falls below their knees: Once they get out the door they rip that off only to reveal a miniskirt.

—*ROBERT HARRIS*
LOS ANGELES, CALIFORNIA
26 17

OH, ALL RIGHT

My daughters were begging me to let them get their navels pierced at 15. Some of their friends already sported their own piercings; many others were not allowed. They already had a few earlobe piercings, so my anxiety wasn't about the physical "damage" of a navel piercing; more the sexual connotation of it. I also felt that once I allowed them to do that, what would be next—eyebrows, tattoos? Still, after stalling as long as possible, I took each of them to a reputable place and they both got their belly buttons pierced. But I made it clear to each of them that this was going to be it, and that just because I allowed this did not mean nose rings were in their future. I had them each pay for their own piercings and their own rings. I made certain they learned how to manage and clean the area so there would be no infections. In addition, I stipulated that one infection equals the closing of the piercing.

—*C.C.*
NORTHPORT, NEW YORK
16 16

I REMEMBER LOOKING UP at my six-foot-two, 16-year-old son soon after he came home from a school trip to New York and seeing that he was wearing earrings. I was furious! I knew he was physically bigger than I, but he knows that I'm the boss. I said, "You take those earrings out right now!" And you know, he did.

—*BARBARA STEVENS*
GATLINBURG, TENNESSEE
47 45 44

• • • • • • • •

"**My older son *says* he wants a tattoo; I don't quite believe it. He also wants to be a pro soccer player. I've told him when he gets his first professional contract, he can go spend his first check on a tattoo.**"

—*BARB*
LOUISVILLE, KENTUCKY
16 15 8

• • • • • • • •

MY GIRLS LOVE TO SHOP: I was no less clothes-obsessed as a teen. The one thing that has cut down on shopping (and spending money) is that my girls also get a kick out of wearing some of the clothes that I wore in my twenties, after they found my low-waisted bell-bottoms and some hippie shirts in the attic.

—*MONICA I.*
SAN FRANCISCO, CALIFORNIA
17 14

DON'T GO SHOPPING WITH YOUR TEEN: Every time my daughter asks me to go shopping with her, we get into an argument. She'll say, "I found something really cute, and I want your opinion." No matter what I respond with, however, it bugs her. Why does she ask me to go with her in the first place if she isn't going to listen to my opinion?

— *M.D.E.*
COLUMBIA, MISSOURI
😊 *36* 😊 *21* 😊 *19*

. . . .

OTHER THAN FOR VERY SPECIAL EVENTS, teenage girls should not be wearing makeup. Girls of that age have such natural beauty that they shouldn't cover it up. No matter what their friends are doing, you just have to say no.

— *JOAN PIERSON*
CRANBERRY TOWNSHIP, PENNSYLVANIA
😊 *25* 😊 *23*

. . . .

I SURVIVED MY SON'S blue, green, orange, red, and yellow hair between eighth and tenth grades. I really didn't see a problem. It didn't hurt anyone. After the first shock wore off, I even helped him dye it sometimes. But the worst was when he cut himself a Mohawk last spring at the end of his sophomore year in high school. It was so ugly and scary I literally couldn't look at him. I told him truthfully that I didn't like it, but I didn't have a fit. He shaved his head after about a month, which was better. And now his hair is about an inch and a half long, his natural, dark-brown color, and it looks good. His girlfriend, however, had her hair cut into a Mohawk a few weeks ago. It looks darling on her, because she doesn't spike it, just lets it fall. Or am I mellowing already?

— *JUDY*
WISCONSIN
😊 *24* 😊 *16*

OLDER AND WISER

My son dyed his hair black and pierced his eyebrow, nose and tongue. At first I was shocked, wondering, "What's going on?" Then I was angry, and then a bit embarrassed: people begin to look at him as if he came from Mars. I felt as if I had done something wrong.

I soon realized the more I got on his case and tried to change his ways, the more he changed. I complained about his black hair, so he dyed it purple: I complained about him piercing his nose, so he pierced his tongue and eyebrow. Eventually, I learned to embrace this time as a maturing experience, and learned to allow my son to find himself. Most of his actions were fads and I knew he would outgrow them. It was very hard to not criticize him, but as his mother I needed to be on his side, not against him. I knew that others would make fun of him, and I didn't want to be one of them. I hoped that one day he would realize that in searching for himself, he did not have to make such radical changes.

And in fact, that turned out to be the case. After about a year my son realized that looking so opposite was hindering his ability to get a job, and others had begun treating him differently. I had tried telling him these things, but he had to learn on his own. He did learn, and came back to his old self a bit wiser.

—*Tricia Novak*
Oaklyn, New Jersey
23

I BRAINWASHED MY DAUGHTER: From the time she was a young child, we would see girls dressed provocatively and I would say, "Honey, look at that girl with her yucky tummy hanging out. And look at you, your tummy is not hanging out. You look so pretty dressed the way you are." And she grew up thinking this is pretty and the other thing is not. My daughter always dressed respectably.

—*TINA COY*
  SAN DIEGO, CALIFORNIA
  22 *20*

• • • • • • • •

MY DAUGHTER WANTS TO HIGHLIGHT her beautiful dirty-blonde hair. I tell her that each time you color your hair, it gets coarser to the point where it will be extremely frizzy by middle age. I point out my sister-in-law, who has highlighted or colored her hair since she was a teenager. Now age 40, she has very frizzy hair and it's not pretty at all. I'll bet she would now say she wished she hadn't put all those chemicals in her hair when she was a teenager.

—*H.S.*
  GOLDEN, COLORADO
  14 *12*

• • • • • • • •

MY HUSBAND ALWAYS WARNED MY KIDS that if they got a tattoo, they'd be thrown out of the house. When my daughter got one, she confided in me and for the benefit of the family I told her not to tell her dad. Although I didn't feel comfortable with it and normally don't keep big things from him, I had no choice. No matter how much you tell kids not to do things, they will ultimately do what they want.

—*S.F.*
  BUFFALO GROVE, ILLINOIS
  22 *20*

TEEN TOPIC

Teens spent an estimated $170 billion in 2004.

Don't lecture. It only makes the idea of getting—or keeping—a weird piercing or tattoo more appealing.

—*STEVEN GREEN*
LOS ANGELES,
CALIFORNIA
👧 *35* 😊 *30* 😊 *29*
😊 *25* 😊 *17*

WHEN MY SON WAS IN EIGHTH GRADE, he came home one day with a spiked Mohawk and his head shaved on both sides. Naturally, he hadn't asked permission, so we made him wash it out. Not long after that, he had Field Day at school. The school secretary called my wife at least three times during the day, asking her to please bring my son a hat because his shaved head kept getting sunburned. My wife's response? "Good! Maybe he'll learn."

—*JOE HOLLIMAN*
CENTENNIAL, COLORADO
👦 *29* 😊 *27*

• • • • • • • •

MY TEENAGE DAUGHTER HAD red, green, blue— you name it—hair. She hung out with a lot of artistic friends. I figured it was a temporary thing. I was just happy she didn't have any tattoos or a ring in her nose. I did threaten her that if she ever got a tattoo I would take her to a doctor and have it removed, and it wouldn't be fun.

—*L.M.*
FALMOUTH, MAINE
👧 *35* 👧 *35* 😊 *29* 👧 *23*

• • • • • • • •

LET'S FACE IT: As a parent, your opinions on things like makeup are worthless to your kids. Luckily, there are many teen magazines out there, and you're bound to find at least one that gives the advice you want. I figured out which magazines my daughter considered the "best" sources of fashion info, then scoured them for articles about how "less is more" and how the natural look is in. Then I just casually left the magazines open to those pages. She actually did start wearing less makeup after that campaign.

—*JILL H.*
NEW YORK, NEW YORK
👧 *14* 👧 *12*

BETTER LIVING THROUGH OFFICE SUPPLIES

I was in a meeting at work when my son called. My employer knew it must be important, because my kids didn't usually call me at work, so they put the call through to the conference room and my son said, "You know, I've been wanting to get my ears pierced." I said, "Yes . . . ?" He said, "And we have this electric staple gun downstairs. Do you supposed if I used that . . . " So I calmly said, "No, no, a staple gun would not be good for piercing your ears. The staples are likely to go into your cranium and that would not be good. When I get home we can talk about it and we can go get your ears pierced." I got off the phone, turned to everyone, and shrieked "Oh my God, a staple gun!" And they said, "You were so calm!" But you have to be calm in those situations. And the funny thing was, my son never did get his ears pierced. I immediately took him to the kiosk in the mall to do it, but he just shrugged it off.

—PEG
DENVER, COLORADO
29   25

MY CHILD WANTS TATTOOS and several piercings. I told her to wait until she is 18 for the piercings and she can pay for them herself. I told her we would discuss the tattoo on her 16th birthday. Heck, I might even pay for it.

—*RITA PORTER*
SPRINGFIELD, MISSOURI
14

" I never really got the thing where parents get so upset about hair styles or colors. I mean, if you ever had a mullet you should just keep your mouth shut no matter what your kid's hair looks like. "

—*KADESH HARDIE*
FROSTBURG, MARYLAND
16

THEY'RE GOING TO DO ALL KINDS OF CRAZY THINGS to try to express themselves, or distinguish themselves as different. As long as they are not hurting themselves or others, I say let them do it, no matter how you may feel about pink hair. Soon they will have a strong sense of self, and they will *know* how unique they are. They won't feel the need to prove it all the time.

—*ANNE SMALLEY*
WOODBURY, NEW JERSEY
19 15

I TOOK MY SON SHOPPING FOR JEANS one time and couldn't figure out what he wanted. Everything I pointed out to him was wrong or "dorky." I realized you just have to give them the money to buy their clothes and then just deal with it.

> *—J.R.*
> *IOWA CITY, IOWA*
> 15

• • • • • • • •

WHEN WE FEEL OUR TEEN IS REBELLING against our parental authority in any form, we try to find the root cause of it. Rebellion is usually a symptom of something that's awry. Sometimes it can be simply that the teen wants more freedom, or sometimes he is angry about something. Teens don't always know what's bothering them or causing them to act out the way they do. Helping them see this can bring them to a place where they see the problem and see there is hope to work through it. Once the root cause is identified, we try to help him with it. If he is trying to honestly work it out, there is usually no consequence. If he continues with the rebellion, then the consequence is related to the rebellion but usually involves restriction in his activities and privileges.

> *—CINDY PRESCHER*
> *REDMOND, OREGON*
> 25 22 19 15

• • • • • • • •

WHEN MY DAUGHTER FIRST BLEACHED out her beautiful hair to dye it hot pink, I was horrified but I didn't show it, and I'm glad. It was shocking, but it wasn't harmful, and it wasn't dangerous behavior. The way I look at it, at least she didn't have her private parts pierced.

> *—NAOMI NEMTZOW*
> *NEW YORK, NEW YORK*
> 22 16 16

WHAT'S REALLY FUN

Teenage girls rank shopping, going to the beach and even sleeping late above dating on their list of things to do.

My son said that he was going to shave off all his beautiful hair. I replied that I thought he would look good bald because he had a nice-shaped head. He kept his hair.

—J.T.
SANTA CRUZ,
CALIFORNIA
31

MY DAUGHTER HAD ALWAYS BEEN really good about makeup. She never wore too much, and I respected her for that. Now that she's gone away to college, however, she looks awful: Her eyes are really dark and black, as though she's outlined them with a marker. Her features just can't carry that. Her father and I decided the best way to handle this was to treat her and myself to a day of beauty. We're going to go to a salon and have pedicures, manicures and professional makeup application. Of course, there's a hidden agenda for us, but we're not trying to be mean about it. I know her well enough to know that the second she takes one look at her "new" self, that's all she will need.

—P.O.
NEW BRUNSWICK, NEW JERSEY
18   15

· · · · · · · ·

BE CAREFUL ABOUT JUDGING A KID by his appearance. One of my son's best friends from grade school radically changed his appearance in junior high. He dyed his hair rainbow colors, which changed every week, pierced more body parts than I'd like to think about, and began wearing black T-shirts with frightening messages and chains hanging from every pocket. He remained the same sweet kid he'd always been, though. At 22, still purple and pierced, he'll be the first in his family to graduate from college, and he plans to become a high school French teacher. The kids will love him. If I hadn't known him so well as a young child, I would have worried a lot about my son hanging out with him. What a mistake that would have been!

—S.S.
SARATOGA SPRINGS, NEW YORK
22

HOLEY COW!

Our kids attended a small private school which began to feel restrictive. So they started hanging out with kids from other schools and going up to Harlem and to other places in the city. My daughter became one of those people who gets everything pierced and tattooed. Whenever she'd get her hands on any money, she'd come home with another pierced body part. It was horrifying to watch, and each new instance was a fait accompli: We couldn't monitor her every minute, and she'd simply come home with a tongue stud or something. She didn't stop even when she had a nostril  pierced down in Greenwich Village and it got infected and her nose blew up like a balloon. My husband had to rush her back there to have the stud removed. But we realized that our kids' way of individuating themselves was to move outside of their sheltered environment and become part of the larger city. And you have to hold on to the thought that kids do mature, and although my daughter still loves her tattoos, with the exception of a couple of extra rings in her ear, she no longer has pierced body parts.

—SALLY EVANS
NEW YORK, NEW YORK
29 23

WHERE TO HAVE FUN

Sixty-eight percent of 12- to 19-year-olds spend time at the mall in any given week. On average, teens spend 3.5 hours at the mall each week.

DON'T SWEAT THE SMALL STUFF. When my son was in the ninth grade he wanted to cut his jeans to three-quarter length and fringe them. I helped him do it. He wore them to school and the principal's office called and told me, "Ms. Duvall, jeans are not allowed to have fringes on them." I told them I didn't understand why not. This experience showed my son that school might not give him his personal freedom, but his parents will listen to him and support him. As a result, he's talked to me about sex, relationships, and even asks me questions. If I hadn't been as open a parent and worked with his likes and dislikes, then that openness wouldn't be there. Besides, there are so many bigger issues than clothes that teens have to deal with, including drugs, alcohol, and committing to school. Your children need to be able to make good decisions without you. You can start by giving them enough room to grow.

—*MIMI DUVALL*
CANYON LAKE, TEXAS
25 23 23 11

It: Teens & Sex

*S*ex: *More than drugs, fashion, or church attendance, it's the subject that can make a confident parent feel like a pompous hypocrite when dealing with teenage offspring. The only relief is that talking about sex embarrasses both teens and their parents equally. But talk you must, as many parents will advise in this chapter. For more uncomfortable details, read on.*

DATING IS NOT LIKE IT USED TO BE. Kids go out with other kids in groups. The formal dating thing is something that doesn't exist in the world my kids live in.

—B.S.
BROOKLYN, NEW YORK
22 17

> **DON'T BE AFRAID TO TELL YOUR TEENS WHAT YOU EXPECT OF THEM.**
>
> —DOLORES JOHNSON
> WICHITA, KANSAS
> 50 48 45

My 14 year old was making statements about sexual matters, acting very all-knowing, and I called her bluff, but gently: I said, "I don't think you really know what you're talking about." She replied, "Well, I wish I did."

—N.
BROOKLYN,
NEW YORK
17

WHEN MY OLDEST SON was in eighth grade he had his first girlfriend. I think that means he would walk her home from school and they would talk on the phone at night. I remember when they broke up, I felt so bad for him. She left him for a boy who was entering tenth grade. It's hard for a mom to watch that—unrequited love. But having that experience is natural.

—K.S.
SAN FRANCISCO, CALIFORNIA
27 22

MY DAUGHTER HAS A STEADY BOYFRIEND and I don't know what they do when they're alone together. I used to agonize over it, and I tried giving her some lectures, but you could tell that just turned her off. Finally, I had to accept the fact I couldn't control her. What I could do, however, was try to remain accessible by refraining from nagging or criticizing her. It's hard, but I try to withhold judgment whenever I can, because that only shuts her down and prevents her from confiding in me.

—M.C.
DENVER, COLORADO
16 13

ALLOWING YOUR TEENS to go out on dates means that you trust them enough to act responsibly on their own. Dating is a healthy, important part of growing up—interacting with the opposite sex on a more intimate level than ever before (I'm not talking about sex here!). Teens need this interaction to learn more about themselves and the person they are becoming.

—COLETTE GABOR
PHILADELPHIA, PENNSYLVANIA
14

PUT IT IN WRITING

It's so important to talk with your teen about relating to the opposite sex. I actually put my advice to my son in writing. I wrote:

"You're beginning to make a lot of girl friends. That's good, but there are ground rules that apply to girls that don't necessarily apply to boys. Call it Girl Etiquette:

1. Be yourself and don't create an alter ego.
2. Always be respectful.
3. Always be complimentary.
4. Do not tease a girl or make fun of her in any way; of course, the same applies to your guy friends.
5. Don't Touch. Unfortunately in today's society, touching is taboo.

Love, Dad"

> —AL PARISI
> AGOURA HILLS, CALIFORNIA
> 🧑21 👦16

MY TEENS WERE RAISED in a religious house, which made it easier for us to impose rules. There is protocol around issues like dating— there was a standard set by our community that we tried to adhere to. Our kids didn't question it, because other teens at their religious school had to follow the same rules.

—*JOHN SYRTASH*
THORNHILL, ONTARIO, CANADA
😊21 🧒17 😊17

· · · · · · · ·

" **When you ask teens about sex, and they say, 'Gross,' they're lying. They're all doing it and if they're not, they're wishing they were.** "

—*K.S., PEDIATRIC/ADOLESCENT NURSE*
BALTIMORE, MARYLAND

· · · · · · · ·

MY DAUGHTER'S A MAGNET FOR LOSERS. The boys she's attracted to are so different from us, it makes you wonder if you ever taught her anything. There was one person whom she had to sneak around with because she already knew we wouldn't have liked him. If she were more upfront about her choices in men and let us get to know them, it wouldn't be any big deal. It sure is something you don't think about when you're changing her diaper.

—*JANE*
BROOKLYN, NEW YORK
🧒16 😊2

MY 14-YEAR-OLD DAUGHTER recently started dating. For some reason, her 15-year-old boyfriend is intimidated and seems to be downright scared of my wife, which we all find hilarious. She is a very gentle soul, but she is also the disciplinarian of the house, because I spend a fair amount of time traveling for work. We talked about it, and decided that we'll just let him feel that way for a while—there may come a time when it works to our advantage.

—*DAVE W.*
PHILADELPHIA, PENNSYLVANIA
14

· · · · · · · · ·

I KNOW THIS PROBABLY MAKES ME a bad father but I had a much more difficult time when my daughter started dating than when my sons did. As a man you tend to be much more protective of your girls. I know I was rude to some of the boys she brought home for no reason other than they were dating my daughter.

—*B.L.*
POLAND, OHIO
41 39 35 29

· · · · · · · · ·

BOYS HAVE TO LEARN that they must respect you and obey your rules. I remember one night my ex-wife called me, hysterical because our daughter, who was 16 at the time, wasn't back from her date and it was getting really late. I went over to the house. When her date arrived I probably scared him a little, but I said, "Young man, don't you ever bring my daughter home past midnight again. You knew the rules and don't you disrespect us like that again." And man, he didn't either. I don't think he asked her out again, but that was fine with us.

—*B.*
GATLINBURG, TENNESSEE

Chain your teenage daughter to her room. It will keep her from going to clubs. It's better to be on the safe side.

—*B.C.*
HELOTES, TEXAS
30

THE SEX TALK, FOR PARENTS OF BOYS

WE HAD A CODE THAT WE USED WITH OUR BOYS: KYPIYP, which stood for "keep your pecker in your pants." This was our humorous way of beginning a sex conversation. The lighthearted introduction immediately made both us and them feel more comfortable.

> —*JOAN K. HITCHENS*
> *CENTENNIAL, COLORADO*
> 32   28

WHEN MY SON WAS A JUNIOR IN HIGH SCHOOL, I came home unexpectedly one day and found an empty condom wrapper lying on the floor by the garage. Later that night, as the two of us were eating dinner, I pulled out the condom wrapper and threw it directly into the middle of his tuna casserole without saying a word. He looked shocked, but honestly, we ended up having one of the best, most open talks we'd ever had about sex.

> —*TINA KUNZER-MURPHY*
> *LAS VEGAS, NEVADA*
> 21

MY TALK WITH MY SON WAS JUST ONE OF THOSE THINGS we did when he was going into high school. It wasn't a sex talk, per se: It was more "the ways of the world" sort of thing. He started going out more and we didn't know where he was every waking moment. I told him, "You need to wear a condom. That's the bottom line. Not only to protect against disease, but you don't want to have a baby. And you need to treat girls with respect. If they say no, that means no."

> —*GARY S.*
> *TAMPA, FLORIDA*
> 17   13

I TOLD MY SON TO GET SOME CONDOMS AND PRACTICE; they were harder to use than he might think. He listened to that!

—*S.S.*
SARATOGA SPRINGS, NEW YORK
22

• • • • • • • •

YOU HAVE TO BE BRAVE. We started talking to our boys about sex when they were young. We also talked with them about the importance of using condoms. When we thought my older son was becoming sexually active, he was still living at home. We wanted to make sure he had protection. I remember talking with my husband about who would have that talk with my son—"You do it!" "No, you!" We agreed that my husband would talk to him. He went to my son and offered, "Do you need anything—some condoms? You can use our charge at the drugstore if you want!" It was funny at the time—but both our sons did use the charge to buy condoms at some point.

—*F.M.*
LONG BRANCH, NEW JERSEY
28 25

TEEN TOPIC

One of every three teenage girls has had sex by age 16. Two out of every three teenage girls and boys have had sex by age 18.

DADS ESPECIALLY NEED TO HAMMER HOME the message to their daughters that they are pretty, and that guys really prefer real girls to supermodels. This isn't something to start saying when your daughter's a teenager. Say it early, say it often, and your daughter will really internalize at least some of that message! Our daughter is remarkably self-confident, and I hope I've helped with that.

> —J.W.
> ROCHESTER, NEW YORK
> 😊 13 😊 13

• • • • • • • •

I WISH SOMEONE HAD WARNED ME there would be a weird double standard in the way I deal with my son and daughter. You tell your son to go out, have a good time, and don't bring home any grandchildren. When it comes to your daughter, however, you're extremely overprotective of her because you don't want anybody looking at her with lust in their eyes the way *you* used to with other women.

> —ROBERT HARRIS
> LOS ANGELES, CALIFORNIA
> 😊 26 😊 17

• • • • • • • •

I HAD TO PUSH TO HAVE THE TALK with my teenage son. He was curious about sex but didn't want to ask me. He hinted around. So I sat down with him and talked to him about male functionality—erections and wet dreams and certain urges. I was very straightforward, and we would get to a point where it would be too much information and he would say, "I don't want to know about it." And I would say, "Fine" and walk away. And he would say, "Wait a minute. Tell me about that."

> —ANONYMOUS
> ATLANTA, GEORGIA
> 😊 14 😊 12 😊 5

I REQUIRE A **"FATHER INTERVIEW"** with any guy who wants to date my daughter. She escorts the young man upstairs into my office, where I have strategically placed the "boyfriend board" in plain view (pictures of me doing SWAT training, shooting weapons, yelling at recruits, etc.). After she leaves, I tell the guy to think of dating my daughter like playing baseball: You can bunt, you can run to first, but there will be *no* home runs, and if you attempt to round the corner and head to second, you'd better watch out, because you're going to meet me. I'll admit it: The purpose is to scare the hell out of the kid. I know what most guys are all about. Nothing is going to stop them from thinking with the wrong head except a mean, intimidating father.

> —*KERRY MCINTOSH*
> *CASTLE ROCK, COLORADO*
> 😊 *25* 😊 *23* 😊 *21* 👧 *20* 👧 *19* 👧 *5*

• • • • • • • •

BEFORE A BOY WOULD COME OVER to pick up my daughter for a date, she would say, "Please Daddy, do not give him the look." But you have to check them out; it's your duty as a father. Pay close attention to how they act when they arrive. I always looked them in the eyes and shook their hands, and I always figured that if they'd look me in the eyes they were all right. And if they wouldn't come to the door, she wasn't going back out the door with them.

> —*JEFF KANE*
> *HOCKESIN, DELAWARE*

Lay down very concrete rules before your child becomes a teen. My daughter knew at 10 what ages she was going to be able to "group date" and then "single date." Now there are no challenges to this rule, because she has been hearing it for years.

> —*KIMERA BROWN*
> *CLEVELAND, OHIO*

THE SEX TALK, FOR PARENTS OF GIRLS

IF YOU HAVE A TEENAGE DAUGHTER, lock her in the closet until she is 25, then let her out and allow her to talk to boys on the phone. When she reaches 30, it is pretty safe to let her physically come into contact with the opposite sex. As a father of a 27-year-old daughter and another daughter on the way (yes, at 53 years of age), I have concluded that this is the best way for a dad to safely bring a daughter from her teenage years to adulthood. But if locking your teenager in a closet is not an option, then you must be a parent that your teen feels comfortable talking with: This is accomplished not by being her friend, but by being a friendly parent.

—*D.N.*
EUREKA SPRINGS, ARIZONA
🌼30 🌸27

• • • • • • • • •

I THINK TEENAGE GIRLS SHOULD HAVE birth control sprinkled on their cereal. When my older daughter was about 16 or 17, I thought she might be sexually active, since she had a steady boyfriend. I asked her, "Do you need birth control?" She said no, she didn't need it, and seemed embarrassed that I asked. When she went to the doctor, I called him and asked him to find out if she needed birth control. He asked her, and she accepted.

—*L.*
BEJOU, MINNESOTA
🌼32 🌼31 🌸30 🌸27

MY 14-YEAR-OLD DAUGHTER NEEDS TO LEARN never to
pick up a drink—whether in a glass or
can—that she's put down or had out of her
sight for a moment. I also tell her that
guys always want what they cannot have.
But mostly, I just encourage her to be herself.

>—*ALLISON T. LEVYN*
>*BEVERLY HILLS, CALIFORNIA*
>   *21   21   18   14   14*

• • • • • • • • •

I GOT SOME ADVICE ONCE ABOUT DAUGHTERS. I was told they can grow
up to be promiscuous as teens if they've never had a man in their life
showing them affection and love; no man telling her how proud he is
of her, that she's pretty. As my daughter got older, I started having
regular date nights with her. I treated her like a gentleman should. I'd
give her flowers. I'd give her a card. It's made her more confident.

>—*J.G.*
>*LYNCOURT, NEW YORK*
>   *21   18   14*

• • • • • • • • •

YOU HAVE TO REMIND YOUR DAUGHTER that she will remember her
sexual experiences and partners for the rest of her life.

>—*CYNTHIA LOVE*
>*SANDSTON, VIRGINIA*
>   *20*

I DON'T WANT MY 17-YEAR-OLD SON and his girlfriend in my house without anyone there. Sometimes that works. He says, "Where can I be alone with her?" It's a good question. But he understands.

> —*RICHARD GLUCK*
> *ATLANTA, GEORGIA*
> 👶17 👶16 👶12

• • • • • • • •

❝My sons kept the dating part of their lives very private, but I knew when they were in love, and when they had their hearts broken. I suppose it was a mother's instinct, and also the fact that they would occasionally tell me.❞

> —*DEEDEE MELMET*
> *SONOMA, CALIFORNIA*
> 👶35 👶32 👶30 👶28

• • • • • • • •

MY WIFE AND I WERE VERY PROUD to tell our kids that we were high school sweethearts and how special it was that we saved the gift of intimacy for each other. You can't be shy about talking to your teens about it, or beat around the bush. Ask questions, but if the first question you ask is, "Are you taking birth control pills?" it's too late.

> —*AL PARISI*
> *AGOURA HILLS, CALIFORNIA*
> 👧21 👶16

BY THE TIME OUR KIDS were old enough to need to know about sex, they'd already found out about the birds and the bees at school. That was nice because we could wait until they asked about things. They'd come home from school and when we were talking about their day, they'd say, "We saw this film in class, and it was gross." That gave us a chance to talk about it on their terms.

—*ANONYMOUS*
GAMBRILLS, MARYLAND
😊 *38* 😊 *36* 😊 *30*

• • • • • • • •

WHEN MY DAUGHTER WAS ABOUT 15 YEARS OLD, she met a young man I did not approve of at all. He had dropped out of school, didn't work, had long hair, and a bad relationship with his parents. A lot of other parents told me I should not insist she stop seeing him but try to reason with her. I should suggest that she not spend all her time with him, see other people as well, and follow some rules about curfew. I shouldn't be too harsh on her and her relationship with this person. Unfortunately, I listened to all of these well-meaning people, and did let this relationship continue. One evening I came home, only to find this young man and my daughter sleeping, hav-  ing enjoyed a very healthy dose of pot. I woke them up, threw him out of the house, flushed the rest of his pot down the toilet, and grounded my daughter for an extended period of time. I told her she was not allowed to ever see him again. The end result? A few weeks later, she thanked me for taking a stand. She had started to become very confused about the whole relationship, and really did need guidance. So, the situation improved by using tough love and discipline.

—*N.S.*
TAMPA, FLORIDA
41 😊 *36*

I'm a science teacher, so when I talk about sex I use very big words.

—*Denise L.*
Chicago, Illinois
13

I tell my sons, "You're only in high school once. You don't get a second shot. You don't want to waste your time on a two-year girlfriend. You need to try other things, other people, other girls, other social situations. Don't get bogged down. You don't have to marry your high school sweetheart. You don't have to love everybody." My son has been dating the same girl for over six months. Having a girlfriend longer than six months is a waste, I think. I'm pushing him hard to break up with her. It's a sensitive topic. I spin it in a positive way. I say, "She's nice and I like her, but you're not going marry her. You need to get out there and try other people."

—*Anonymous*
Atlanta, Georgia
16 12 10

One night, my daughter, who was 16, came in and said, "Well, tonight, Mary is sleeping with Joe and last weekend she slept with John and tomorrow night it will probably be Mike." As a parent, you think, "Oh, my God." But you have to say only, "Oh. How does that seem to you?" Instead of making judgments, step back and ask them how it seems to them. They're usually going to come up with the right answer.

—*Pat Williams*
Atlanta, Georgia
21 19

When my kids were younger the AIDS epidemic was just coming to light. I told them, "I just want to tell you one thing. If you get a girl pregnant, there's a choice. If you get AIDS, there is no choice. You die."

—*Caren Masem*
Greensboro, North Carolina
33 28

IF YOUR TEEN COMES OUT . . .

MY DAUGHTER IS GAY. She came out in a formal letter to her mother and me when she was 19. Immediately, we called her at college to assure her we still loved her. To us, there was never any question about this. Other parents who might be struggling to accept their child's sexual orientation should remember that we're all God's children. If you loved your child before he or she came out, you should still love your child afterward.

> —*JOE HOLLIMAN*
> *CENTENNIAL, COLORADO*
> *29 27*

FIRST OF ALL, I WOULD TAKE CARE to let him know that being gay is not a disease and that I love him regardless of whether he is gay or straight. I would sit down and talk to him, listen to him, and let him know that while the path he's chosen may be difficult because of others in this world, I will give him my full support and understanding.

> —*B.*
> *COLORADO SPRINGS, COLORADO*
> *14*

HUG HIM and tell him you love him.

> —*D.S.*
> *VICTORIA, BRITISH COLUMBIA, CANADA*
> *22 19 12*

DON'T WAIT TO HAVE THE SEX TALK; have it before you think they need it. Start when they are young and answer every question they have. And remember, at any age they know more than their parents think they know. I learned that teaching sex education in high school. All you can give them is the information and the background on the choices. Tell them, "You are going to have make choices when I'm not there to help you."

—*DOLORES JOHNSON*
WICHITA, KANSAS
🐍 50 😊 48 😊 45

• • • • • • • •

MOST KIDS WANT THEIR PARENTS TO KNOW they're sexually active—they just don't want to admit it. So they leave subtle clues, like staying out much later than curfew and neglecting to have their friends cover for them. One day, a friend of mine came home and saw her daughter and her daughter's boyfriend sitting together on a bed: She just knew. You have to keep your eyes open for clues like these.

—*E.C., WORKS WITH TEENS AGED 15 TO 19*
NEW YORK, NEW YORK

• • • • • • • •

HAVE THE FULL TALK ABOUT SEX *before* your kids are teenagers. They're more awkward at that age, and embarrassed, and it's harder to be matter-of-fact. When they're younger, you can really lay it all out and even if it seems "gross" to them, they'll get it. Then, when they're older, you only have to update a little of the information to make it appropriate for their age, but the foundation is already there.

—*DEKE*
SAN DIEGO, CALIFORNIA
🐍 13 😊 10

NEVER, EVER TELL YOUR DAUGHTER to stop dating a particular boy! My daughter dated a boy for six years because I constantly told her that I didn't like him. I don't think she liked him very much either, but she had to prove that I was wrong. I should have just kept my mouth shut and allowed her to make the decision for herself.

—*SUE*
DESTIN, FLORIDA
24 15

· · · · · · · ·

'Sometimes it's hard to remember that what is happening at the moment with your teenagers seems monumental to them, but it is really just transient and will often blow over quickly. **"**

—*ANONYMOUS*
REDMOND, WASHINGTON
29 26 21

· · · · · · · ·

I FOUND WITH MY SON that the easiest way to get started talking about sex was to use a story that perhaps was on the television news or in the newspaper. There are always stories about sexually transmitted diseases, date rape, or something similar. If you have a current event to start off with it makes the entire conversation go more smoothly.

—*SHIRL MAWHINNEY*
PORTERSVILLE, PENNSYLVANIA
13

TEEN TOPIC

Three-quarters of teens surveyed use some method of contraception (usually a condom) the first time they have sex.

MY SON WAS MADLY IN LOVE with this one girl and all of a sudden she said, "I don't want to do this anymore. You're smothering me." He thought he was doing everything he was supposed to do and it backfired on him. We sat down and we talked, and he cried and I cried. I hated as a kid hearing my parents say, "You'll go through 50 women before you find the one you want." So I tried to talk to him about it. "What do you think happened?" It wasn't just one time that we talked; it was a half dozen times over a month or so. He would let things out and leave and come back later and talk about it. I told him, "Relationships are probably the hardest thing you have to deal with in your life."

—*GARY COLLINS*
TAMPA, FLORIDA
17

* * * * * * * * *

WHEN MY DAUGHTER TURNED 16, she came to me and said she wanted to be put on birth control. I was in tears for about two weeks, but with mixed emotions. I was happy that she trusted me enough to tell me, but I was also faced with the sharp realization that she wasn't our little girl anymore. When I spoke with my gynecologist, she said my husband and I should be proud of how we raised our daughter, and that most parents don't have the luxury of having that chat. We told our daughter about the birds and the bees when she was very young, and it was always a very healthy discussion. My parents always said, "If there's no communication, then there's a problem." We've always had that communication, and it has been a wonderful thing.

—*H.*
COATESVILLE, PENNSYLVANIA
31

I WAS WORKING IN A HEALTH CLINIC when my
children were teens. So with my boys, I took
home a bag full of condoms one day and set it on
my buffet in the dining room. I was a single mom
at the time, and they didn't want to talk to me
about sex. The bag disappeared, and I felt better.

—*S.*
TRAVERSE CITY, MICHIGAN
*28 *26 *24*

**"Read the notes in his backpack:
That's how I found out my
brother's secrets and what
was really going on with his
girlfriend. Be snoopy. "**

—*K.K.*
CHICAGO, ILLINOIS
23

WHEN MY OLDEST SON WAS 16, he developed a
urinary problem, so I took him to his pediatrician
who told me he had venereal disease. My first
thought was, "Oh, my God! I need to sit him
down immediately and talk about safe sex." I'd
been planning on doing this before he left for
college, but the STD incident woke me up to the
reality that the time to start talking about sex is
much, much earlier. I wished I'd started when he
was about 12 or 13.

—*S.G.*
LOS ANGELES, CALIFORNIA
*35 *30 *29 *25 *17*

I NEVER, EVER TALKED TO MY SONS about sex. I wanted to portray the image of the mother who was to be respected, so I didn't watch explicit movies, listen to explicit lyrics, or talk about explicit things with them. I'll admit this was chancy and I wouldn't advise everyone to try it. But I was the only woman living in a household with four boys and a husband, and I felt uncomfortable bringing up sex. Besides, my sons had plenty of friends and other sources to learn about those things from.

—*JANIS HACKETT*
CENTENNIAL, COLORADO
36 *32* *26* *24*

"Get teens to take care of a toddler for a week. That should be enough to discourage them from having unprotected sex."

—*TAMARA*
LOVELAND, COLORADO
3 *1*

WHEN MY OLDEST WAS A SENIOR IN HIGH SCHOOL, she started dating a guy we *knew* was a druggie. We really had to be careful to not make him more attractive to her by forbidding her to see him. Instead, we just kept a really watchful eye on her to make sure that she wasn't getting sucked into his world. It worked!

—*P.M.*
TULSA, OKLAHOMA
30 *27* *25*

I **TALK ABOUT SEX VERY DIRECTLY** with my sons. All the changes with boys start around the eighth grade. And I've found the girls are much more aggressive than boys at that age. I would always say to my sons, "Hey, you're going to be sitting at a concert with a couple of your friends and girls are going to start holding your hand and put their head on your shoulder. My rule is, nothing below the neck: NBTN. You might end up kissing a girl, but that's all you need to be doing right now." They would go away to summer camp and I would sign their letters, "NBTN, Dad."

—*RICHARD GLUCK*
ATLANTA, GEORGIA
🌀*17* 🌀*16* 🌀*12*

• • • • • • • • •

MY DAUGHTER GOT PREGNANT TWICE as a teenager—the second time, she had the baby. I made her take complete responsibility for herself and the baby. She had to get a job, pay rent, hire a babysitter, and handle all the responsibilities of adulthood. It was very difficult to watch her and refrain from solving her problems. After all, I wanted to help my daughter and granddaughter. But I knew that if I helped her too much, she would just continue to act irresponsibly and keep having babies. She had a hard time, but eventually she was able to finish school, get a job, and take care of herself and her child. I'm very proud of the person she's become. In some ways, she resents the way I treated her in those days, but I know she would be a different person if I had not been tough on her.

—*M.*
VALLEJO, CALIFORNIA
🐾*35*

Our sex discussions were usually held in the car on the way to visit family in Indiana. My husband and I were honest with our girls and answered every question. We agreed to use real words and not euphemisms.

—*DEE*
OAK LAWN,
ILLINOIS
🐾*29* 🐾*24*

SEX, ABSTINENCE, PREGNANCY, STDs, AIDS—you name it, we've had the discussions. I listened to one son regret his loss of virginity while we sat together for two hours. Although he was 19, he was visibly disappointed and I helped him deal with his choice. I listened to another express disappointment at a girl with a high sexual desire who tried to strip down at every chance. I've heard about girls who have strange habits and the temptations the boys try to avoid. We allowed snuggling when they had girls over to their rooms, but made it clear the room was open for our inspection at any time. I even joked at times, calling out, "You guys still got your clothes on in there?" The girlfriends seemed to enjoy the attention and respected our wishes because we were "cool." We started early having open discussions and we've counted our blessings ever since.

—*C. HOPE CLARK*
PHOENIX, ARIZONA
31 26 21 19

Only Rock 'n' Roll: Media, Technology, & Your Teen

F ace it: You're getting old. You've seen the teens with their cell phones and their MP3 players and their IM and their whatchamacallits. You've watched the videos and movies, with their overtly sexual messages and skimpy costumes. You've heard those awful lyrics. If you don't understand any of it—well, you're not alone. But, if you desire peaceful coexistence with your music-and-tech-savvy child, read on.

MONITOR THEIR INTERNET USE. My kids are never online without permission and supervision. How do I know for sure? Because they don't know the password!

> —DEB UHLER
> HELLERTOWN, PENNSYLVANIA
> 14 10

IT'S A GOOD IDEA FOR TEENS TO HAVE CELL PHONES TO USE IN EMERGENCY SITUATIONS.

> —BONNIE LAMB
> CHICAGO, ILLINOIS
> 23 20

TEEN TOPIC

The best-selling video games are rated M (Mature). They are extremely popular with pre-teen and teenage boys, who report no trouble buying the games.

IN THIS AGE OF "CLASSIC ROCK," you can get their attention once in a while by saying something like, "Well when I saw Led Zeppelin in Philadelphia. . . . Or, "I can't remember if I saw the Dead six times or seven . . . " They can't quite get their heads around it, but for a moment or two, you have transcended complete parent-nerd-turd status.

—*E.T.*
PORTLAND, MAINE
17 13

• • • • • • • •

COMPUTERS ARE SUCH A VITAL COMPONENT of all aspects of modern life. Parents should encourage and allow their kids to experiment with computers and Internet use. I don't think it's a good idea to limit them.

—*MARTIN SEABECK*
FOMBELL, PENNSYLVANIA
21 20

• • • • • • • •

USE CALLER ID TO YOUR ADVANTAGE. My son had a friend who was bad news. Every time this kid called our house, his dad's name would show up on our Caller ID and we refused to answer it because we didn't even want the two of them to talk.

—*L.A.*
CLEVELAND, OHIO
23 21

• • • • • • • •

WE HAVE TWO SONS AND ONE DAUGHTER. Originally, we had given the girl her own land phone line; but with time, we found good cell phone plans that included free evenings. This saved us from fighting over using the phone.

—*JOHN SYRTASH*
THORNHILL, ONTARIO, CANADA
21 17 17

I DON'T BELIEVE KIDS SHOULD HAVE CELL PHONES, except to make sure they have a way of contacting you. When I was growing up you had money in your pocket to phone your parents to let them know where you were. The oldest scam in the book was, "I couldn't find a pay phone." I gave my son a cell phone specifically to stay in touch with me. It's like having a pay phone in your pocket.

—*GARY COLLINS*
TAMPA, FLORIDA
😊*17*

• • • • • • • •

GET RID OF TV; for a while, anyway. When we moved to a new home a few years ago, we didn't get around to having our cable hooked up. It was March, so nice weather was coming, and the kids would be outside playing. We finally got the cable hooked up in October. This was such a positive experience, that we have our cable turned off every year between April and October. This way, my kids play outside more, and we don't miss the reruns a bit. My kids still have their computer games and movies to watch, so they don't complain about missing TV. By doing without cable, we save more than $40 a month. I spend that extra money on season tickets to an amusement park and water park a few minutes away.

—*DEB UHLER*
HELLERTOWN, PENNSYLVANIA
😊*14* 😊*10*

• • • • • • • •

PARENTS NEED TO HAVE A CELL-PHONE PLAN that doesn't count minutes when it's a cell-to-cell call. I never wanted my children to say to me, "We didn't have enough minutes to call you." This way, I can call them and they can call me at no cost.

—*KAREN*
KNOXVILLE, TENNESSEE
😊*17* 😊*14*

Don't compare your child's teen culture to your own, and don't belittle it. I had one child who was a rebel and one who was conservative. I never told my rebellious child to change her clothes. I let all my kids be who they wanted to be.

—*APRIL ROBINS*
ELLISON
SAN ANTONIO,
TEXAS
😊*24* 👧*21* 👧*21*

THE INTERNET AND YOUR TEEN

I DO NOT CENSOR THE INTERNET or any other part of life. My children have very good judgment and quite a bit of wisdom. I discovered that my daughter had been reading erotica on the Web (I had to laugh at this) and I know my son has looked at "those" sorts of pictures. Filtering these things out would just mean that if they wanted to find it they'd have to go elsewhere. It doesn't really keep children from objectionable materials. I firmly believe that growing up involves learning to set your own limits. If a person can't learn how to do that, he will have big trouble in life.

—*G.B.*
LOS ANGELES, CALIFORNIA
21 *14*

. . . .

WITH SO MANY YOUNG MEN IN THE HOUSE, we have strict computer rules and we use filters. The family computer is out in the family room where everyone can see the monitor. We don't allow computers in the bedrooms. We don't allow the computer on if neither Dad nor I are home. We closely monitor the history of Web sites visited and we check over his shoulder when our son is using the Instant Messenger. We have a password to his e-mail and we randomly check his e-mail account.

—*CINDY PRESCHER*
REDMOND, OREGON
25 *22* *19* *15*

. . . .

MY SON IS IN FRONT OF THE COMPUTER TOO MUCH, in my opinion. It's tough, because we do not live in a neighborhood where there are kids, and his options are limited for free time. I tried to filter the Internet, but the program I installed caused more problems than ever. Luckily for us, he is into sports more than porn, so the great majority of his time online (to my knowledge) is playing sports games.

—*TOBY LYNN*
ATLANTA, GEORGIA
14

WE DID NOT ALLOW OUR TEENS to have computers in their bedrooms. Our family computer sat in the middle of the living room so that they wouldn't be tempted to bring up a picture they wouldn't want others to see. One stepson spent time in a chat room. Although he was just 14, he claimed to be 25 and would be "honored to be the father of your children." He told the young woman that he was going to Nebraska to visit an aunt the next month, and would meet her there. How did I know what he was doing? I opened the cache in Netscape afterwards (not sure if IE has the same function), and read every word that he typed.

—*DIANE EVANS*
RENTON, WASHINGTON
30 28 26 26 25

· · · · · · · ·

COMPUTERS ARE PART OF LIFE NOW, and not an issue. When she was younger, I had parental controls put on her AOL account and discussed online safety with her. When she was 18, I lifted the controls, confident that she had learned responsible computer use.

—*ANGIE MANGINO*
STATEN ISLAND, NEW YORK
27 25 19

· · · · · · · ·

MY DAUGHTER HAS A FRIEND SHE TALKS TO on the Internet. They met about a year ago at a state softball tournament. He looks exactly like Harry Potter. His e-mail address is written next to the computer for all to see. There's nothing hidden. We have a laptop on the dining room table. If you write something someone shouldn't see, everyone *will* see it.

—*CHIP NORTON*
WASHOUGAL, WASHINGTON
13

TEEN TOPIC

One of the growing uses for mobile phones among youth is video games—now at about $100 million in annual sales and expected to double by next year.

DON'T GIVE THEM A CELL PHONE, unless they are going to be driving a long distance or driving very late at night (and they shouldn't be doing that anyway). I just can't get over how many kids today walk around with these phones stuck to their ears at all times of day and night. Who are they talking to? Each other, of course. The cell phone is a great invention, but the average teenager does not need one in her regular everyday life.

—*SANDRA MONROE*
CUMBERLAND, MARYLAND
23 19

• • • • • • • •

WE HELD OFF ON GETTING THEM CELL PHONES until high school. Most parents today see it as a safety feature: They get it in case their kid is stuck somewhere. Of course, that's not what the kids are interested in. You give them the phones so you can reach them, but they don't have to answer it. In one month on my daughter's bill there were 400 to 500 phone calls and 100 text messages. Text messages, to them, are just as easy as breathing.

—*L.C.*
YARMOUTH, MAINE
16 14 11

• • • • • • • •

I NEVER REALLY UNDERSTOOD THIS, but it seems that there are online video games that you can play with friends. My son and his friends took turns going to one another's houses to play this particular game. It involved taking your own computer to the host house. Seemed like a lot of work to me, but it kept them out of trouble and from roaming the streets. There are a lot worse things to be addicted to.

—*TERRI*
TROY, NEW YORK
25 24 22 21

WHEN MY DAUGHTERS WERE TEENAGERS, I didn't permit them to play computer games or listen to a Walkman at the dinner table. On occasion, we'd read, but usually we tried to just enjoy our meals and talk. My wife actually once played computer games at the table: this didn't thrill me, either!

—*ANONYMOUS*
ALLENTOWN, PENNSYLVANIA
🐶*33* 🐶*31*

• • • • • • • • •

' Don't be afraid to use the phrase, 'I will take away your computer/TV/Nintendo/phone if you don't follow my rules.' Use technology as a weapon for good behavior. ' '

—*K.H.*
LIBERTYVILLE, ILLINOIS
🌐*18* 🐶*13*

• • • • • • • • •

I USE IM AT WORK A LOT WITH CO-WORKERS, so I can IM the same as my sons, although sometimes they tell me I am using the wrong acronym. I like it when they get home from school and I see them from work on IM. I can talk to them in real time—"Get dinner going" and "Did you do your homework?"

—*KAREN*
GREAT DIAMOND ISLAND, MAINE
🌐*16* 🌐*14*

WE HAVE HBO IN THE HOUSE and there are risqué movies on there. There's raunchy stuff on cable at eleven o'clock. And I noticed that my son kept going to the basement to watch TV. We put a lock on the TV so you have to enter a code to watch it. When we told him all he said was, "Oh."

—*DANIEL*
   ATLANTA, GEORGIA
   14 12 5

THE NUMBERS DON'T LIE

- Average time per week that the American child age 2-17 spends watching television:
  19 hours, 40 minutes

- Time per week that parents spend in meaningful conversation with their children:
  38.5 minutes

- Hours per year the average American youth spends in school:
  900

- Hours per year the average American youth watches television:
  1,023

- Chance that an American parent requires children to do their homework before watching TV:
  1 in 12

IN OUR HOUSE, you can't answer your cell phone or text message at the dinner table. We try to take the phone off the hook during dinner.

—*RICHARD GLUCK*
ATLANTA, GEORGIA
🌀*17* 🌀*16* 🌀*12*

• • • • • • • •

IN ONE MONTH WE HAD A BILL for 700 to 800 text messages on his cell phone. I teased him—"Do you ever *talk* to anyone anymore?" It's funny, because talking is free, but text messaging costs money.

—*GARY COLLINS*
TAMPA, FLORIDA
🌀*17*

• • • • • • • •

HAVING ONE COMPUTER AND FOUR TEENAGERS made for some intense family moments. The oldest fell in love with Macs and saved up enough to buy his own computer. Of course he constantly reminded us of the superiority of his product anytime we had trouble with the PC. Whenever we asked any questions about the computer, his response was always, "Get a Mac." He got a job teaching the younger kids at school how to use the computer and made enough money to further upgrade his system. The rest of us had to take turns using the other computer. Having access to the personal computer is one of the benefits of the kids moving out of the house!

—*TERRI*
TROY, NEW YORK
🌀*25* 🌀*24* 🌀*22* 🌀*21*

• • • • • • • •

WHEN MY DAUGHTERS WERE TEENAGERS, we were careful about the TV and movies they watched. They didn't see any R-rated movies.

—*ANONYMOUS*
ALLENTOWN, PENNSYLVANIA
🌀*33* 🌀*31*

Be open-minded. Don't write off their music or their favorite television shows or their friends just because they are different than what you liked at that age. Give it a try.

—*SANDRA FONKOUA*
SILVER SPRING,
MARYLAND
🌀*14*

WHEN MY SON BECAME ENCHANTED with rap music, he would turn it down voluntarily when I came close. He knew I really disapproved of the foul language and misogynistic lyrics of rap, so that was the one move he made to not annoy me.

—*C.W.*
BOULDER, COLORADO
👧 22

. . . .

❝ I've been very lucky with my son, but he does listen to dreadful rap music or whatever today's version of Metallica is called. And he's been taking electric guitar lessons since the beginning of the year. I spend a lot of time yelling, 'Turn it down!' ❞

—*MARY MEDLAND*
BALTIMORE, MARYLAND
👧 14

. . . .

THE RULE IS, the oldest generation in the car has to be OK with the music—whether it's me, my wife, or the visiting grandparents. On short rides, the kids can deal with it. For long rides, letting them have their own Walkman or MP3 player is essential.

—*M.S.*
NEW YORK, NEW YORK
👧 18 👦 13

I RECALL ALL TOO WELL my own Led Zeppelin days versus my parents' Sinatra days. Today, of course, I much prefer Sinatra. I keep this in mind whenever my teens listen to their music around me. I cringe at my Caucasian daughters' tastes, as they prefer black urban rap to anything else. We've had our share of battles in the car, and when the lyrics get offensive, I change the station.

> —*C.*
> *NORTHPORT, NEW YORK*
> 🧒 *16* 🧒 *16*

• • • • • • • •

WHEN IT COMES TO ROCK 'N' ROLL, there are only slight variations on the basic theme if you listen closely enough. Your kid's rock is basically your rock changed just enough so they feel rebellious. Give it a serious listen and don't be dismissive. You'll be surprised how much you like it.

> —*HELEN HUGHES*
> *CLEVELAND, OHIO*
> 👧 *28* 🧒 *21*

• • • • • • • •

I DON'T LET HIM LISTEN TO RAP MUSIC in my presence because the majority of it is demeaning to women. I don't like the language, and I don't like it when the rappers refer to their girlfriends as whores.

> —*GARY COLLINS*
> *TAMPA, FLORIDA*
> 👧 *17*

• • • • • • • •

I USED TO GO TO CONCERTS with my son when he was 13 and 14. We enjoy the same type of jam bands. We went to Dave Matthews. But, after a while, they don't want Dad around. I understand: Sometimes I don't want me around, either.

> —*ANONYMOUS*
> *ATLANTA, GEORGIA*
> 👧 *16* 👧 *12* 🧒 *10*

TEEN TOPIC

Teens in families with home computers and Internet access spend much less time watching television— about seven hours a week less. They also spend more time studying.

IT'S INSTANT MESSAGING. They don't use the phone anymore, really. Two of my children are very, very social and they are on IM all the time. They can chat with many different people at the same time. I'll tell you, they are great typists. They can type faster than you can imagine.

—*L.C.*
YARMOUTH, MAINE
👧 16 👧 14 👦 11

• • • • • • • •

WE'RE A TECHNO-FAMILY: the more technology the better. My sons don't e-mail at all. It's just too slow. It's all about IM and text messaging: they are married to their cell phones and text messaging. But they will never sit down and write an e-mail.

—*RICHARD GLUCK*
ATLANTA, GEORGIA
👦 17 👦 16 👦 12

WHAT DO TEENS DO ONLINE?

- E-mail: 56%
- "Chat": 53%
- Get homework help: 51%
- Surf the Net: 45%
- Play games: 42%
- Sample and listen to music: 35%
- Download music and audio files: 35%
- Get information about things they'd like to buy: 34%
- Instant messaging with buddies: 29%
- Get information on hobbies: 25%

MY SON WAS REALLY INTO BUYING SONGS. His generation is used to paying 99 cents for a song. He would ask for my credit card. One month I got my credit card bill and I saw $50 in songs on it. When I told him, he said, "I didn't realize I bought that much." So I got him a Visa Buxx card through the bank. It acts and looks like a Visa card and I put $10 every two weeks on it. I can put extra money on it if he's done something like babysitting. You can see exactly what he's spending money on. It gives us some semblance of control. And now he's much more conscious of how much he is spending.

—*ANONYMOUS*
ATLANTA, GEORGIA
🌝*14* 🌝*12* 🌝*5*

FORBIDDEN FRUIT

Teenagers who say their parents restrict their television viewing of certain programs are likely to watch the forbidden shows at the home of a friend, according to a recent study. They also reported less positive attitudes toward their parents. But parents who discuss issues related to TV with their older children —rather than just restrict watching—are more likely to influence what their offspring watch. The key, says Ohio State University Professor Amy Nathanson, is to discuss without lecturing.

TEEN TOPIC

In a survey
of over 600
parents and
teachers, less
than three
percent had
any knowl-
edge of the
anti-female
content of
some video
games.

NOWHERE IS IT WRITTEN in the Constitution that
you have to provide your teenage daughter with
her own phone line. Parents need to understand
this because she will certainly act like it's her
constitutional right. However, it's actually smart
to install two phone lines for a couple of reasons.
One, so you can actually have telephone conversations yourself. Two, because it gives you more
power. If your daughter stays out past her curfew,
for example, you can actually follow through on
your threat to shut off her phone without inter-
rupting your own activities.

> —*W. BRUCE CAMERON*
> *SANTA MONICA, CALIFORNIA*
> 👧 *22* 👧 *20* 👦 *20*

• • • • • • • •

WE DON'T ALLOW VIOLENT VIDEO GAMES in our
house. Yes, my sons have played them at other
people's houses. But guns and shooting—not
in my house. They play the NCAA sports video
games.

> —*KAREN*
> *KNOXVILLE, TENNESSEE*
> 👦 *17* 👦 *14*

• • • • • • • •

ONE THING I DO TO CONNECT with my teens is
watch some of the television shows that interest
them, either when we're together or sometimes
when I'm alone. For example, I often tune into
The Real World on MTV. I know this is something
they watch and talk about with their friends, and
I like to be part of it. Also, sometimes, when
their friends are over they'll come into my room
and catch me watching that or another teen-ori-
ented show. Their friends think I'm cool, and I
score points with my daughters.

> —*C.C.*
> *NORTHPORT, NEW YORK*
> 👧 *16* 👧 *16*

My son has had a TV in his room since he was 11 or 12. He played a lot of video games, and I never would have been able to watch my shows if I hadn't let him have his own TV. That said, I do think it was a mistake: It allowed him to exclude himself from family activities more than I would have liked. My daughter tells me that it's not fair that her brother has a TV and she doesn't, and I just say, "Well, I'm sorry, but that's the way it is." She doesn't play video games and does like to be with us, and I want to keep it that way.

—*Anonymous*
Littleton, Colorado
😊19 🐾13

• • • • • • • •

If you ban music at home that you don't want your kids to listen to, that doesn't help; they will hear it somewhere else. We actually talk about rap lyrics in our home and point out disgusting or dirty things we hear in the music to our kids. I'd rather help to form opinions than just clamp down with rules.

—*V.P.*
Mundelein, Illinois
🐾21 😊18 😊15 😊12 😊7 🐾5

• • • • • • • •

My oldest fought to see R-rated movies since he was in eighth or ninth grade—all his friends wanted to see one, and I just said no. The other people paying to go see that movie do not need a bunch of 14-year-olds behind them watching it, too. I just said that there are plenty of good PG-13 movies that are out there so, pick from them. I finally let him go to R-rated movies when he was 15. What changed my mind? I see him as a very mature teenager.

—*Barb*
Louisville, Kentucky
😊16 😊15 🐾8

TEEN TOPIC

Sixty percent of teens admit that a celebrity idol had influenced their attitudes and personal values, including their work ethic and views on morality.

Pray for them a lot!

—Bob C.
Springfield,
Illinois
😊33 😊28 😊25
😊21

EVERYBODY NEEDS THEIR PRIVACY, but don't have computers, TVs or phones in your teenager's bedrooms. If you do, they'll spend all their time there and grow up away from their family. Go so far as to put the family computers in one room. That way everyone is together even if they're busy at work or play.

—Rosetta Hammond
Louisville, Kentucky
😊39 👧36

• • • • • • • •

I DIDN'T HAVE THAT MANY PROBLEMS with my teens' music because I was a disc jockey. They liked the Beatles; I liked the Beatles. Even if you don't understand the music your teens like, try to find an interest you can share with them. It helps your relationship.

—John Powell
Earlysville, Virginia
😊43 😊42

• • • • • • • •

WHEN MY WIFE OR I would notice our kids watching something questionable on TV, instead of yelling, "Turn that off," we'd ask, "Do you think that's age-appropriate?" More often than not, our son or daughter would say, "No," and turn the channel.

—Al Parisi
Agoura Hills, California
👧21 😊16

Do As I Say: Teens, Alcohol, & Drugs

Are you experienced? Have you ever been experienced? Careful how you answer that: Your teen is listening and applying your responses to her own life. It's all part of the difficult phase that every teen and parent faces—dealing with alcohol and drugs. On the one hand, teens need to make their own decisions eventually. On the other hand, it's your job to protect them. Read on for advice.

THOSE COMMERCIALS THAT TELL YOU to talk to your kids about drugs—they are right! I always thought it would be really uncomfortable and awkward to do that, but it is definitely effective.

—ELLA JEFFE
NEW YORK, NEW YORK
😊 17 😊 13

TEENAGERS HIDE STUFF: IT'S PART OF THEIR JOB DESCRIPTION.

—KELLY DIXON
KIRKLAND,
WASHINGTON
😊 23 😊 16 😊 16

TEEN TOPIC

The percentages of eighth- and tenth-graders using any illicit drug are at their lowest levels since 1993 and 1995, respectively.

JUST STOP AND THINK ABOUT what you did as a teenager before you pass judgment on something they did. Our daughter was caught drinking in high school. What we did as a way of punishment was make her write a five-page essay on alcoholism. I can't say it stopped her from drinking, but she sure knew what alcoholism was.

—B.D.
CORALVILLE, IOWA
🙂31 🙂28 👧25

• • • • • • • •

WHEN MY DAUGHTER WAS 17, she came home from a concert. It was late, and normally I wasn't up when she came home, but this night I was working on a project. I noticed that her eyes looked funny. I asked, "Have you been drinking?" At first she said, "No," but then she said, "Yes." I'm happy to say I didn't freak out and get crazy. We sat down and had a quiet talk. I expressed my concern for her safety, and I talked to her about trust. I think she reacted in a positive way to the way I didn't scream and yell—that I treated her like an adult. But she was grounded anyway.

—W.S.
WAYSIDE, NEW JERSEY
🙂26 👧24 👧18

• • • • • • • •

WHEN MY SON WAS A TEENAGER, we would do little scenarios; like: "If you are at a party and your friend is drinking beer and the police come, you are guilty by association." I would also tell him, "You can party all night but you don't have to drink or have sex to have a party." I never had problems with him. Later, when he went to college, I told him, "I'm sorry I was so strict with you." He told me, "I didn't miss a thing."

—VELMA O. WILLARD
BOERNE, TEXAS
🙂23

I SUSPECTED MY OLDEST SON was using marijuana, so I told him there was a test I could buy at Walgreen's that would prove it for sure. His eyes grew wide and he immediately confessed. He had no idea I was making it up, but I knew the only way I'd get the truth was to scare it out of him. It's a very effective technique.

—*L.H.*
  HOUSTON, TEXAS
  😀 *17* 😀 *16* 👧 *15* 👧 *14* 👧 *12*

. . . .

❛❛I had my daughters sign a contract vowing that if they were drinking at a party, they would call Mom or Dad and we would pick them up, no questions asked.❜❜

—*CAROL KWIATKOWSKI*
  MILLTOWN, NEW JERSEY
  👧 *27* 👧 *27*

. . . .

I DON'T GET SO UPTIGHT, the way many parents do, about my son trying things like marijuana. They have to live and learn. The important thing is that we talk about it. I feel that we can talk about anything, nothing is off limits, and I think he feels the same way. Afterward he can say, yeah, I tried that but I didn't like it. I think it makes for a much healthier relationship than just telling them that certain things are bad before they even try it.

—*ANONYMOUS*
  SOUTH BEND, INDIANA
  😀 *13* 👧 *8*

A LONG ROAD BACK

Iknew that my son had tried marijuana off and on since the summer between eighth and ninth grade. How? A police officer called a home where we were chaperoning a teen party to tell us that my son and two other kids had been caught smoking marijuana in the park down the street. Were we embarrassed and mad about that! We hadn't noticed that he had left the backyard, even though we were watching the kids, mainly for signs of drinking. He was grounded and had his phone taken away, and he knew he was in big trouble.

I thought he had learned his lesson, but the summer after tenth grade, we had to put him in an outpatient drug and alcohol treatment program for adolescents. It met three times a week for three hours and required us to make a contract with consequences for unacceptable behavior. He always threatened that he was not going to go to the next meeting, and he got up and walked out during the first family-night meeting. But he came back and stuck with the program, finishing it after eight weeks and following up with one hour a week of aftercare and with AA or NA meetings once a week on his own.

Most of the teens in the treatment program were in for marijuana addiction. He has made new friends from the treatment group. None of them are perfect, but they are sweet, funny, and touchingly sensitive to each other as they try to focus on staying clean one day at a time. We are proud of our son's effort and of our own involvement in his treatment program. Things are calm now, but we will continue to seek help when we think he needs it.

—J.
WISCONSIN
 24 *16*

ONE NIGHT, MY SON WENT OUT with some friends; he then called and said he was spending the night with a friend. Late that night, however, he came home and said he needed to pick up a couple of things and then he was going back to his friend's house. However, it was obvious to me that he had had several beers and was in no condition to drive. When I explained this to him, he didn't respond well. Well, there was no way I was going to let him drive that car! When he went up to his room, I proceeded to hide every car key I could find—for his car, my car, and any car in the vicinity! I had a feeling that after I went to bed he was going to sneak out! The next morning (pretty early, as I recall), when I came into the kitchen my son was sitting there. He apologized for everything he had said. Tough love, I like to think, kept him out of the car, and made him realize that he used inappropriate behavior. And I discovered that morning that my son's friend had been in the car when my son drove home—and he had slept in the car the whole night!

> If you did it, you can be sure they'll do it.
>
> —*P.J. WHITE*
> *LOS ANGELES,*
> *CALIFORNIA*
> 🌐 22 👥 9

— *NOLA SMITH*
TAMPA, FLORIDA
👥 41 🌐 36

• • • • • • • • •

I DON'T DISAPPROVE OF DRUGS. At my daughter's high school, a lot of the kids smoke pot. It became apparent to me that she would smoke pot soon. And so I told her to smoke it at home, instead of out in the street where she could get arrested. I'm not going to be a hypocrite. I actually lost a friend because I was letting the kids smoke pot in my house. He didn't want his kid smoking pot. But there are certain things you have to be savvy about. They are going to do it anyway.

— *B.S.*
BROOKLYN, NEW YORK
🌐 22 👥 17

STARTING WHEN EACH KID REACHED AGE 9, whenever we'd have wine or beer with meals, I'd pour my kids a small amount so they could taste it (I didn't give them hard liquor). Medically, there's no harm in doing this and, more important, it takes away the taboo. Neither of my kids went through the wild and crazy, "get drunk" phase, because to them drinking was never a big deal.

—*EMMILLIO E.*
VANCOUVER, BRITISH COLUMBIA, CANADA
😊 27 👧 22

* * * * * * * *

"We have an old friend who was put in the hospital for alcohol poisoning. I brought my son to visit and see how absolutely pathetic that was."

—*TOBY LYNN*
ATLANTA, GEORGIA
😊 14

* * * * * * * *

SOMETIMES SOMETHING GOOD can come out of something scary. One night I discovered that my son and his best friend had shared a whole bottle of Wild Turkey. At home. In the bedroom. All in thirty minutes. Although this was a scary time, with thoughts of ambulances and alcohol poisoning, it turned out to be a great deterrent to ever drinking again.

—*SHELLEY*
TAMPA, FLORIDA
😊 17 👧 12

WHEN MY DAUGHTER WAS a high school fresh-man, I found out from another mother that she was smoking pot. This woman said that her daughter and my daughter had been introduced to the drug by a third mother, who smoked it with them. I couldn't believe this. In my day, we had to lie, cheat, steal, and sneak around to do illegal things: We certainly didn't have parents handing them to us! This experience taught me that not only don't you have control over your kids when they're with their friends, but you don't have control over them, *period.* The best defense is to work on establishing an open rela-tionship. Then, when serious issues come up (and they will), your kids will feel comfortable talking to you.

> —*ANONYMOUS*
> *SALINA, UTAH*
> 🧒23 👶19 👶19 🧒17

• • • • • • • •

I HAD TWO BASIC RULES RAISING MY KIDS: Always let me know where you are, and never get into a car with someone drunk. They would call me at 1 a.m. and say, "You've got to come and get me. I can't find anyone who can drive me home." They never got into any real trouble, but I made some trips in the middle of the night to come get them.

> —*LANAN SHELTON*
> *AUSTIN, TEXAS*
> 👶36 👶34

• • • • • • • •

I CAN'T BELIEVE HOW PRISSY AND PRUDISH the parents of my generation have become, consider-ing that many of them participated in Woodstock and with all that generation took part in. It's stupid and insane.

> —*B.S.*
> *BROOKLYN, NEW YORK*
> 👶22 🧒17

TEEN TOPIC

Among high school seniors, Vicodin is the second most frequently reported drug used, after marijuana.

KEGGER AT YOUR HOUSE!

IF YOU GO OUT OF TOWN AND YOUR CHILDREN STAY IN TOWN, even if they stay at someone else's house, they're going to somehow make it back to your house and have a party. So just be prepared.

> —*PAT WILLIAMS*
> *ATLANTA, GEORGIA*
> 🐵 *21* 👦 *19*

• • • • • • • • •

ONCE, MY KIDS WERE WITH ME ON VACATION, and my son's best friend had a party at our house while we were gone. He was supposed to water the plants and change the cat litter. When I came home, things were out of place: There was a tooth-brush in my bathroom that wasn't mine and I could tell that someone had slept in my bed. Then my neighbor called and said, "You might find a lot of beer cans, if you look in your garbage." And I did. So I talked with my son's friend. I said, "I've known you since the ninth grade. You sleep over here. You eat our food. I treat you like my son. I'm like your other mother—how could you do this to me?" He tried to say they had a party someplace else and he brought the beer cans to our garbage can. But he finally admitted to it. And I told his mother.

> —*CAREN MASEM*
> *GREENSBORO, NORTH CAROLINA*
> 👦 *33* 👦 *28*

I WENT OUT OF TOWN FOR THE WEEKEND. My daughter thought she would have a party and invited everybody she knew. After the first two people walked in the door, the two teachers who lived next door were calling me. I phoned home and told her the party was over. "I know what's going on," I told her. "Let's not get into any more trouble: just send them home and we'll talk about it later." She was a bright child, but just one of those kids who got caught all the time. With them, you can nip things in bud.

—ANNIE BRABSON
PRAIRIE VILLAGE, KANSAS
34

· · · · · · · · ·

MY MIDDLE DAUGHTER WAS QUITE A PARTY GIRL. One time, we had to leave her at home because we went camping. Word got out that she was having a party; she had probably 50 people in the house and the yard. Our next-door neighbor couldn't sleep and it was two or three in the morning. He ran over in his underwear, through our house, screaming at everyone to get out. He must have been really aggravated, because he didn't even take the time to put his pants on. So when my son made it to the teenage years, we decided we weren't going to go away at all. It worked. We just parked the trailer in the yard and didn't go anywhere.

—NANCY DISALVO
EXETER, RHODE ISLAND
28 24 20

TEEN TOPIC

Sixty-seven percent of eighth-graders and eighty-three percent of tenth-graders say that alcohol is readily available to them for consumption.

BEFORE THE KIDS GO OUT, I SAY, "No drugs, no drinking." I get the eye rolls and "MooooOOOOooom. *We* don't do that." And most of them don't. But some have been caught. I just add that some day, at some party, it's going to be available. I told them all, "I want you to choose *not* to drink and not to do drugs. But if you do, I want you *not* to get into a car with anyone. Make any excuse you need to, but call me, no matter what time of day or night and no matter where and I will come pick you up, no questions asked. I want you alive with me instead of dead because you were afraid of what I'd say."

—*BARB*
LOUISVILLE, KENTUCKY
🌻*16* 🌻*15* 👦*8*

• • • • • • • •

I DON'T THINK MOST PARENTS ARE AWARE of how common drug use is, especially in kids as young as 12 or 13. And it's not just the stoners who are doing it, either—it's all types of kids. I'm a teacher and I had two cheerleaders tell me recently they regularly ditch class to get high.

—*MARK CRANE, HIGH SCHOOL TEACHER*
AURORA, COLORADO

• • • • • • • •

I WAS A HIPPIE, and I smoked pot and did Quaaludes and ate magic mushrooms when I was younger. So I just sat them down, my daughter and stepdaughter, and I said, I've done these things, and I know what they feel like. Drugs make you think that no one can tell you are high and that you are very intelligent. They *can*, and you aren't.

—*CYNTHIA LOVE*
SANDSTON, VIRGINIA
👦*20*

WHEN YOUR TEENAGE DAUGHTER is traveling with you in Europe, she will undoubtedly enjoy her first public beer. Therefore, you should make sure you know the German words for "fish livers in cream sauce." Otherwise, your slightly tipsy daughter might order such a dish and you may end up having to share your own dinner.

> —JIM
> ATLANTA, GEORGIA
> 🐵 35

· · · · · · · ·

'Don't be in denial. There is no such thing as a perfect teenager. All teens are going to drink; just hope that they won't drive. '

> —ANONYMOUS
> CHICAGO, ILLINOIS
> 🐵 24 🐵 20 🐵 19 🐵 17 🐵 15

· · · · · · · ·

I HAD ASKED MY SON MANY TIMES if he was doing drugs, or if he was stoned, and he always said, "No." I guess I just wanted to believe him. But I got a call from him at school that he had been caught off campus with a friend who had pot on him, and that my son knew he had the pot. Still, the experience as a whole was a good one for us. I think my reaction—I didn't freak out and was most angry that he got suspended from school and was missing out academically—spoke to him. We're closer than ever now. But I don't kid myself anymore that I know my child as well as anyone.

> —ANONYMOUS
> KIRKLAND, WASHINGTON
> 🐵 23 🐵 16 🐵 16

My generation experimented a lot: I'm not going to be hypocritical.

> —DEB S.
> SAN DIEGO,
> CALIFORNIA
> 🐵 21 🐵 13

TEEN TOPIC

By the time they leave high school, about 50 percent of kids have tried an illicit drug. Among high school seniors, 39 percent have used an illicit drug in the past 12 months.

YOU CAN'T STOP TEENAGERS from going to parties where alcohol is present, but you can prevent drinking and driving by offering a backup plan. My parents always gave me $20 to keep in my wallet when I was going out, which I thought was the coolest thing in the world. On one hand, it showed that they trusted and respected me enough to let me live my own life. On the other hand, it subtly told me they cared about me while hinting that there are right and wrong ways to handle a situation.

—*RACHEL WALASKAY*
SEDALIA, COLORADO
11 8

• • • • • • • •

GO TO A FAMILY THERAPIST if you feel things are getting out of hand with your child.

—*CARMEN TURNER*
NEW YORK, NEW YORK
15 13

Forging a New Relationship: Late Teens

*L*ook! Up ahead! There's a clearing! It's civilization! Yes, once lost in the jungle of the teen years, you've almost found your way back. But here's a warning: After so many years in the wilderness, don't be surprised if things are different when you return home. Specifically, your teens are different. They are almost—dare we say it?—adults. Onward! A few more steps and you're there.

RIGHT BEFORE THEY GO OFF TO COLLEGE, they're going to get mean and nasty because they have to separate. They have to believe that you are so rotten that they must leave. I had that happen with both of my kids. You just have to know this is the way it's going to be.

—CAREN MASEM
GREENSBORO, NORTH CAROLINA
33 28

KICK THEM OUT AT AGE 13, THEN LET THEM BACK IN AT 24!

—CINDI
SPRINGFIELD, ILLINOIS
33 19 17
16 12

NO MATTER HOW YOU TRY to influence your teenagers, you can't. They already are who they are. You shouldn't despair when they alienate you completely. Because if you let them go to discover whatever it is they have to—even the bad stuff—they're going to come back, as our three now adult kids have, with a huge amount of love, friendship, and three times the loyalty you thought was lost.

—*TOM W.*
LENOX, MASSACHUSETTS

• • • • • • • •

BE PATIENT! You won't know what they have learned from you until they move away from home. My daughters never took my advice when they lived at home. But now that they've moved away, they constantly call and ask, "How do I remove this stain?" or "How do I make that dish you cooked for my senior-class potluck?" That's so gratifying. Best of all, they sometimes say "You were right, Mom!" But I had to be patient and wait for them to discover life for themselves.

—*SUE*
DESTIN, FLORIDA
👧 24 👧 15

How do I survive my teenagers? By remembering something very important . . . it ends!

—*DAN*
SAN FRANCISCO,
CALIFORNIA

• • • • • • • •

AFTER THEY GO AWAY, after their first year of college, or even at Christmastime that first year, they really appreciate what you've done for them. They realize how much they've taken for granted. My kids definitely did that: They said, "Oh, it is so good to be home." The food was right there. There was a place to do the laundry. As they get older they really do get much more appreciative.

—*F.P.*
PORTLAND, MAINE
👦 32 👦 30 👧 25

My oldest son and I spent about ten years of our lives at odds with each other and not quite understanding why. It wasn't until I took the Myers-Briggs personality test that I understood that my son and I were total personality mismatches. It wasn't that he was trying to undermine my authority, it's that our views of life clashed. From that point on, I understood him a little better. Things between us improved drastically when, instead of nagging him to do things my way, I started saying stuff like, "These are the goals I need you to meet; I'll let you figure out how to get there."

—MICHAEL
SOUTH BELOIT, ILLINOIS
34 32 30 26

Parents always imagine the worst and are sometimes proved right.

—N.
BROOKLYN,
NEW YORK
17

I remember when we dropped my daughter off to college. She was standing by the curb, waving to us. My husband and I were both crying as we drove away because it was like the end of our watching over her all the time. From that point on, she never really came back home to live. It hurts, but you go on. You have to.

—DIANE BLOVET
KENNESAW, GEORGIA
39 36 26

People say how lucky we are that our daughter turned out well, but luck had nothing to do with it. It was plain hard work to be parents who were involved, who believed their job was to parent and not just be their kid's pal. You can be pals when they're grown and making their own choices.

—C.L.
PETALUMA, CALIFORNIA
24

I KNEW MY TEEN HAD GROWN UP WHEN . . .

. . . **I STOPPED FEELING UNCOMFORTABLE EVERY TIME** a steamy love scene came on the television when we were watching it together. When kids are in their mid-teens and something like that comes on TV, you either want to crawl under the couch or change the channel at the speed of light. But when my son was 18 that stopped being the case. I knew that he probably knew more about the birds and the bees than I did. At that point I think *he* started feeling uncomfortable about watching that stuff with *me* in the room.

—*C.S.*
EVANS CITY, PENNSYLVANIA
😊 *18* 🙈 *12*

. . . .

. . . **HE GOT HIS HIGH SCHOOL DIPLOMA.** Up to that point it honestly hadn't occurred to me that he was growing up. I wanted to keep thinking of him as my little boy. It wasn't that the signs of his maturity weren't there for me to see: Heck, he'd been working a part-time job for two years and had been volunteering his time all over town for a year. But once I saw him grab that diploma I knew his days of living under my roof and following my rules were nearly over.

—*TERESA BAXTER*
STRUTHERS, OHIO
😊 *35*

. . . .

. . . **I STARTED ASKING HIM FOR ADVICE,** instead of vice versa. It was mostly advice on things like computer use or the best way to get somewhere. But when your kids are in their early or mid-teenage years you do not typically ask for their advice on anything. Once I found myself turning to him for answers, even relatively innocuous ones, I knew he was grown up.

—*TAMMY NANCIK*
CANFIELD, OHIO
😊 *17*

More Wisdom: Good Stuff That Doesn't Fit Anywhere Else

If ever there was a life experience that defied categorization, it's the teen years. And here's the perfect spot for these out-of-category stories, as well as a place where you can gain perspective. Read on, and know that by reading this book, you have shown that you not only care about your teen, but also you are willing to do what it takes to survive and help them survive. That makes you the best kind of parent.

NEVER LOSE YOUR TEMPER and always try to be joyous and good-humored. They will model your behavior. Above all, have tolerance and help them find their place in the world. Every soul has a mission—help them find theirs.

> —S.S., *COUNSELING OVER 40 YEARS*
> *PASSAIC, NEW JERSEY*
> *FOUR KIDS AGES 23 TO 40*

TELL THEM YOU LOVE THEM. THEY NEED TO KNOW THAT.

> —*CHIP NORTON*
> *WASHOUGAL,*
> *WASHINGTON*
> 13

Parents need to understand that our children are not us. They are separate people with separate skills, views of life and goals. Those approaches have to be looked at and valued. This is the first step to becoming friends.

—*MICHAEL*
SOUTH BELOIT,
ILLINOIS
34 32 30
26

IT IS HARD TO SIT BACK and watch your kids fail, but you have to do that. I handicapped my youngest child; cooking for her, cleaning for her, and doing her laundry, because she is the baby and I wanted to protect her. Now she is not strong or independent. She's gullible, she sucks at driving, and as far as social skills go, she will do whatever it takes to fit in.

—*B.*
SAN ANTONIO, TEXAS
26 25 19

• • • • • • • •

TO KEEP FROM GOING INSANE when trying to deal with your teenagers, talk to other parents. Their kids might be going through the same thing. Talk to people you've known for years: They can say, "Yeah, this is happening, this is kind of normal behavior." And you also need to take time out for yourself every once in a while.

—*PAT WILLIAMS*
ATLANTA, GEORGIA
21 19

• • • • • • • •

I BELIEVE THAT THE PROCESS OF GROWING UP is one of discovering who you are and what your God-given talents are; what you're good at and what you enjoy doing. If your child's discoveries overlap with your own interests, you can have life-enriching memories you may never have the opportunity to replicate once they're out of the house.

—*D.W.*
SAN DIEGO, CALIFORNIA
16

• • • • • • • •

IT'S HARD BEING A PARENT. I don't envy my parents anymore, and I'm not that angry at them anymore.

—*B.S.*
BROOKLYN, NEW YORK
22 17

WHEN THEY'RE JUST KIDS, you walk in the door and you can't shake them from you. Now it's the other way around.

> —*D.B.*
> *ATLANTA, GEORGIA*
> 👶14 👶12 👶5

• • • • • • • •

'Parents need a sense of humor, a lot of patience, and their high school yearbook so they can remember what they were like at that age. "

> —*PAT CURRY*
> *ATHENS, GEORGIA*
> 🐾17 🐾15

• • • • • • • •

I HOSTED A 17-YEAR-OLD JAPANESE exchange student for a year. It was an amazing experience to be instantly responsible for a teenager. It was hard adjusting to each other, but I found her to be fascinating. I learned quickly that the teenage experience is universal. I think it may help parents to keep that in mind. Teens don't do the crazy things they do to torment you; they're just being teens! For example, as we were leaving the house, I would tell her, "Remember to bring your keys." She would quickly retort, "You don't have to tell me again. You already told me." But just a few minutes later, she would say, "Uh-oh. I forgot my keys." She was adorable.

> —*ELLEN*
> *PITTSBURGH, PENNSYLVANIA*
> 🐾17

You have to remember what it was like when you were that age: It's the only way you're going to be able to build any kind of relationship with your teenager.

—*Marcy Childs*
Frostburg, Maryland
👦17 👧11

· · · · · · · ·

❝Keep photos of them as babies and toddlers out where you will see them frequently. It helps you to remember that they once actually wanted to be near you. ❞

—*E.T.*
Portland, Maine
👧17 👦13

· · · · · · · ·

Above all, let your teens know that no matter what they do in this world to you or to anyone, they will always have a place in your home and a place in your heart. Some of my kids' friends  have parents who push them so hard to be so good that it hurts their self-esteem. It makes them think, "If I don't do well and go to college, I am going to ruin my parents' lives as well as my own." I tell my children, "I don't care what choices you make. All I want is for you to be happy."

—*D. Garcez*
Helotes, Texas
👧23 👧19 👦16 👦10

WHEN I WAS AROUND 12 OR 13, I was arguing with my father. In a moment of anger, I told my dad, "I hate you." To my surprise, my dad didn't react at all. He just said, "Well, I'll always love you." My dad's words have stuck in my mind for more than 20 years. Even though I was angry and my dad was annoyed, he kept his cool. His calm words stopped the argument cold. I think that his response was the best a parent can give.

—*A.K.*
ALBURTIS, PENNSYLVANIA

· · · · · · · · ·

THE TEEN YEARS ARE THE TOUGHEST YEARS. Every time your kid goes out the door, you worry. To survive it, try not to worry until you have to, because there's plenty of time to do it when something comes up. You can't just sit at home wondering what might happen. When I got a phone call at eleven at night and my son was in an accident, *then* I started worrying because there was something to worry about.

—*DIANE BLOVET*
KENNESAW, GEORGIA
😊 *39* 👧 *36* 👧 *26*

· · · · · · · · ·

THE BEST THING WE DID for our teenagers was to take them abroad. They learned tolerance and openness for different cultures, people, and languages, particularly when they were in the minority group (Americans living in Japan, for example). Also, it brought our family closer together. And my two sons were and still are best friends. So many wonderful and unexpected benefits came from our decision to live in different countries!

—*LEIGH DOBSON*
TORONTO, ONTARIO, CANADA
😊 *25* 😊 *24*

Be your child's champion. Everyone needs a strong supporter, a cheerleader in her corner.

—*MARY SPRINGFIELD, ILLINOIS*
👧 *21* 😊 *17*

KNOW THEIR FRIENDS, talk to them constantly about drinking/drugging (no, not "how to"), try to know their friends' parents (at least introduce yourself to them via the phone when that seems logical), meet with teachers, enter the school fairly frequently even though your kids beg you not to, and make sure your kids know where Planned Parenthood is and what it offers.

—*E.T.*
PORTLAND, MAINE
17 13

· · · · · · · ·

" Do your best; you're a human being and are going to make mistakes, but ask for forgiveness and go on. "

—*JANE FLEMING ROSENBOHM*
HANNA CITY, ILLINOIS
34 32 29 24

· · · · · · · ·

ALWAYS KEEP IN MIND: This too shall pass. When they begin to attack you for being the problem— for being the cause of *all* their problems—it's natural that you'll be defensive. You have to overcome that and let them have their turn to be angry with you, just like you were angry with your parents. That phase passes. You don't necessarily solve it; it's kind of unsolvable. But you survive it.

—*RACHEL WILLIAMS*
RIVERSIDE, CALIFORNIA
23 21

MY HUSBAND AND I WENT to counseling to get through some rough times, and one woman who really helped us had a chart that showed that the two times people most often get divorced is when they have toddlers and when they have teenagers. I would say that chart is right on. Toddlers and teenagers are both very, very demanding and exhausting.

—ANONYMOUS
    YARMOUTH, MAINE
    16 14 11

• • • • • • • •

TEACH YOUR TEEN TO BE INNER-DIRECTED, not outer-directed. If they are inner-directed, they are not dependent on what others think. They have a sense of self that comes from within. It's important to model this behavior and teach it by example; avoid measuring your own self-worth by comparing yourself to others. There will always be someone with a bigger house, a fancier car, and a higher-paying job. If you're inner-directed, you derive your sense of self from your own inner barometer, one that is not dependent on what others have or what others think. Know who you are.

—LENI KASS
    CHICAGO, ILLINOIS
    15

• • • • • • • •

TEENS NEED TO KNOW THAT there is nothing they can do that will make you stop loving them. They also need you to be their excuse when they're being pressured to do something they'd rather not do, but don't want to look uncool. Our daughters have carte blanche to say, "My totally uncool parents won't let me do that" when they want to get out of a tight situation.

—PAT CURRY
    ATHENS, GEORGIA
    17 15

Never say, "When I was your age . . . ," because they really can't believe you ever were.

—ELAINE FANTLE
    SHIMBERG
    TAMPA, FLORIDA
    41 40 38
    37 32

Raising
teenagers is
like reliving
high school,
only without
the peer
pressure.
Boy, is it fun!

—*Kathy*
Laurel,
Maryland
36 33 30
28

It's important to model healthy behavior for kids. For example, I see so many mothers who are obsessed with their weight, not because of health concerns, but because they are striving to achieve some unrealistic, culturally imposed ideal. I've heard mothers tell their daughters that a key to their popularity—especially with the boys—is dependent on their being thin enough. Instead, show your daughters that you are happy with who you are, you take care of yourself physically, mentally, and emotionally, and don't strive to emulate the airbrushed, perfected images portrayed in the media. Praise your daughters for who they are, not what they look like. Teach them that taking pride in their appearance is important, but being defined by it is a path to unhappiness.

—*Anonymous*
Chicago, Illinois
12

• • • • • • • •

This is what I've learned so far:
1. Let them sleep. Teenagers need more sleep than children do!
2. Hug them. Not necessarily in front of their friends, but every chance you get, hug your teens and pre-teens and tell them that you love them.
3. Praise them. They like hearing it from you.

—*Graciela Sholander*
Fort Collins, Colorado
12 10

• • • • • • • •

With your first teenager, you are always so serious. By the time you get down to the third one, you say, "No big deal." Your poor first kid; in spite of you, he survived.

—*Janet Vallone*
Waymart, Pennsylvania
34 31 27

KIDS GROW UP SO FAST: Don't miss it. I was so busy, working so hard, when my kids were teenagers, that I wasn't a part of it. You only get that shot once. It's such a fine line to walk: on one hand you have to work enough to make enough money to provide for your family: On the other hand you don't want to work so much that you miss out on time with the family that you're working so hard for.

—*ED REICH*
DUBOIS, PENNSYLVANIA
43 38 33

· · · · · · · ·

"Parents who try to make copies of themselves are headed for failure. You can't expect your kids to dress, act, and play golf like you. You can't push your dreams on someone else. "

—*NICK*
DURHAM, NORTH CAROLINA
20

· · · · · · · ·

I DON'T KNOW WHAT A COOL PARENT IS. Kids want someone who acts like a friend, lets them do whatever they want and gives them everything, but that's not parenting. Parenting means keeping an eye on things, watching their health, and not leaving them home alone. No kid considers this cool.

—*LUCIA BOLES*
ST. LOUIS, MISSOURI
53 52

YOU DON'T KNOW WHAT IT MEANS to be a parent until you have teenagers. There is absolutely no skill involved in parenting until you have teenagers. All the rug-rat stuff is nothing. It's when they become teenagers that parental strategy really comes into play. That's what separates the men from the boys.

—*RICHARD GLUCK*
ATLANTA, GEORGIA
🙂17 🙂16 🙂12

. . . .

"One way I've survived the children is laughter; being able to laugh at myself and my own mistakes is always helpful. You're going to make mistakes, but you're not the only one. "

—*ANONYMOUS*
ATLANTA, GEORGIA
👧19 👧15

. . . .

JUST REMEMBER, your mother probably did not like you much as a teenager, but she did love you. It's OK to sometimes feel that you don't like your teenager. Just remember that eventually your 14-year-old will develop into an adult, and the person you once liked (and have always loved) will reemerge as your friend for life!

—*H.N.*
OKLAHOMA CITY, OKLAHOMA
FORMER TEENAGER WHO IS NOW BEST FRIENDS WITH HER MOTHER

FROM ABOUT SEVENTH THROUGH tenth grade, it's important for parents to be in tune with their teen's self-image, particularly if you have girls. You know your kids well enough to know when they're not happy. When my daughter was in seventh grade, I realized she was struggling. Many of her friends were stick-thin girls, and my daughter was a full-figured woman. I decided to take action and put her in a swim club. I told her it was just exercise, something to do. She fell in love with it. Suddenly, this girl who wouldn't even walk to the mailbox was jumping into the pool and swimming forever. Exercise helped her lose baby fat and form a beautiful figure. I remember thinking to myself, "Yes! I've succeeded!" when she stood in front of the mirror one day and said, "Mom, I feel so empowered."

—*DEBBIE REDDEN-BRUNELLO*
TEMECULA, CALIFORNIA
18 16

Every teenager can't be treated the same. They all have different personalities.

—*MARI G.*
AZUSA, CALIFORNIA
15 13

MAKE A CONSCIOUS EFFORT to take a holiday from nagging: Try to break the pattern. Resist the urge to fall asleep at nine o'clock every night and stay up later. They are more open to talking later at night when they know you are making an effort to hang out with them. Read books on becoming a young man or woman to know what they are going through. Stick up for them when they need it. Let them know if they fail at something it is not the end of the world. We all have strengths and weaknesses, we just have to figure them out and that is part of the process. Remember to smile, remember to say I love you, remember to joke around.

—*DANA SEBASTIAN*
SAN FRANCISCO, CALIFORNIA

THE RULES

RULE #1: Teenagers, just like adults, want to be heard. In other words, they need to feel validated. They need to feel that their existence in life is necessary and that, whether or not everyone agrees with them, what they have to contribute to this world is important. One way to validate teenagers is to ask them about their interests, and then really listen to their responses. This shows that you are concerned about what they have to say.

RULE #2: Teenagers need to know their boundaries. This rule is very important, and one that many parents of teens today seem to have forgotten. While teens like to pretend, or think that they have it all under control and don't need the guidance of a caring adult, teenagers are just not developmentally capable of categorically governing themselves. It is important for parents, and for anyone working with teens, to set definite rules and consequences so that teenagers know their limits. This gives them a feeling of safety while venturing towards independence.

> —*Nicky G., High school teacher*
> *Oklahoma City, Oklahoma*

GLANCE THROUGH YOUR OLD YEARBOOK to take a trip down memory lane. It will help you empathize with your teen's awkward moments and will help you know how to be there for him.

—*ANONYMOUS*
BUCKHEAD, GEORGIA
😊 *18* 😊 *14*

• • • • • • • •

" Don't be too judgmental about other parents until you've gone through every age with your own children. It's much tougher than it may appear and everyone has a different way of dealing with it all. *"*

—*KELLI SCHARFF*
SPRINGFIELD, ILLINOIS
😊 *19* 😊 *17*

• • • • • • • •

THE BEST WAY TO GAUGE your success at parenting a teenager is to find out what other people think of your kid. They get to see things you don't see when living under the same roof. If people in general, or specifically the parents of kids he or she hangs out with, tell you your kid is sweet, kind, polite, or intelligent, then you're doing a good job. I remember a waitress at the local Friendly's told me that of all the kids she dealt with, he was one of the nicest and best. I was amazed.

—*JOHN W.*
LONGMEADOW, MASSACHUSETTS

PARENTS NEED PATIENCE to survive their teenagers. If you wait it out, the bad hairstyles, clothes, arguments and habits will slowly disappear and your children will finally appreciate who their parents are.

> —*M.F.*
> *BUFFALO GROVE, ILLINOIS*
> 👧 *21* 👦 *20*

• • • • • • • •

66 Don't underestimate what they know and what they've experienced. Teenagers have opportunities to do things that we presumed they wouldn't get to until much later in life and you've got to be able to address those issues sooner than you would expect. 99

> —*MR. Z.*
> *EVANSTON, ILLINOIS*
> 👦 *18* 👦 *16*

• • • • • • • •

ANYTIME I REALLY NEED to put the hammer down, I threaten to get an earring or something designed to make me look cool. It terrifies him. Someday I may get one of those fake tongue studs and a couple of clip-on eyebrow rings and show up at his school or event!

> —*B.C.*
> *SEATTLE, WASHINGTON*
> 👦 *20*

"YOU GET OUT WHAT YOU PUT IN." That's what my mother told me, and she was right. My husband and I made a point of spending quality time with our teenage girls: being there for them, showing respect to them, and listening to them. They needed time, friendship, openness, values, and discipline, and that's what we gave them. They're adults now, and we still talk on the phone every Saturday, even though we live in different countries!

—*PAT Q.T.*
CALIFORNIA
32 27

- - - - - - - - -

PICK YOUR BATTLES CAREFULLY. Is it *that* important if your 15-year-old son wears the same favorite shirt to school every day or wants to pierce his ear? Or will the world end if your 17-year-old likes his room messy? Believe me, there will be bigger and more important battles to wage farther down the road, and life is far too short to try and control such details.

—*SHELLEY OEHLER*
IOWA CITY, IOWA
22 17 15

- - - - - - - - -

I MADE MY SON THIS LIFE INSTRUCTION BOOK. It told him everything wise that I had learned over the years. On each page is a lesson or a story such as: "wash your car on a Friday afternoon and enjoy your weekend," or "make your bed when you first get up." A lot of my friends really liked it, too, so I made copies for them. It's really special for my son, who is now in college. The last time I visited him, he still had it by his bed.

—*BAKER*
ATLANTA, GEORGIA
20

If you can't stand the answer, don't ask the question.

—*CLIFF JOHNSON*
WICHITA, KANSAS
50 48 45

THE JEWEL IN MY POCKET

I have five children. The first three were pretty easy, but the fourth one nearly put me over the edge. She fought in school; she pierced her own nose; she was caught by police after dark in the local park at age 13, and there were beer cans nearby. But probably the worst incident was when she was picked up for shoplifting at a department store at age 16. My father had worked at Woolworth's for years and taught us that stealing was one of the worst crimes, and here I had failed to ingrain that in my own daughter. I got through those years by constantly telling her that I loved her more than anything; that she was the jewel in my pocket; that whatever happens to her happens to me. It was exhausting, trying to convince her that I cared. But in the end, I think "going strong on the love" really worked. She's turned her life around, and is now in college and doing well.

—ANNETTE G.
LONG BRANCH, NEW JERSEY
26 25 21 20 13

THE BEST ADVICE I EVER GOT as a parent was from a friend when I was struggling with my infant daughter. My friend said, "They give you more than one chance." It really helped me all the way through. Teenagers invariably go through periods when you have to ground their hatred, and it seems as if you've lost them. That little tunnel of teenage years, for hormonal reasons, is really difficult. You think they don't love you, and it's unnerving, and sometimes you burst out with over-exaggerated anger. But if you look at anything you've ever read or seen on talk shows, it's amazing to what lengths children will go to reclaim even the worst relationship with their parents. It's so primal. They want it to work.

—C.G.
RIDGEFIELD, CONNECTICUT
27

Lock your teenager away. Every day they hate you and there is no cure except getting older.

—ROY MOORE
SPRING BRANCH, TEXAS
31 28 17
15 8

• • • • • • • • •

FORM A CLUB OF PARENTS who need to survive teens. My husband and I were in a struggle with our son because he didn't want to follow through on a Bar Mitzvah. Although he had started the preparation, he came and told us that he didn't believe in the things he would have to say. Through our talking with the other parents, my husband realized that he was focused on doing this for his own father instead of his son. This prompted my husband to write a letter to his father saying our son would not be having a Bar Mitzvah, but in arriving at this decision had become a man (which is exactly what the ceremony is for). Afterwards, he let our son read the letter. It had often been tense between my son and husband, but after that experience their relationship changed.

—ANONYMOUS
NEW YORK, NEW YORK
32

THE BEST ADVICE I COULD EVER GIVE the parent of a teenager is that it is a finite period of time. It may take a decade or more, depending on how early they enter adolescence, but *it does end.* And it feels so good when it does. It feels as if you, the parent, have also graduated! You get to breathe normally, sleep soundly, and just relax. You may have lots of gray hair, and wrinkles, but you have earned them. You are a survivor, with some semblance of sanity and humor intact, and they are wonderful, responsible, confident adults. Success all around.

—*C.L.*
PETALUMA, CALIFORNIA
24

SPECIAL THANKS

Thanks to our intrepid "headhunters" for going out to find so many parents from around the country with interesting advice to share:

Jamie Allen, Chief Headhunter

Jennifer Blaise	Ken McCarthy	Pippin Ross
Elizabeth Edwardsen	Lindsey Roth Miller	Chris Starrs
Sara Faiwell	Jennifer Nittoso	Andrea Syrtash
Lisa Jaffe Hubbell	Adam Pollock	Beth Turney Rutchik
Shannon Hurd	Peter Ramirez	Matt Villano
Natasha Lambropoulos	William Ramsey	Jade Walker
Heather Leonard	Kazz Regelman	Sara Walker
Nicole Lessin	Jennifer Bright Reich	Joanne Wolfe
R.M. Lofton	Beshaleba Rodell	

Thanks, too, to our editorial advisor Anne Kostick. And thanks to our assistant, Miri Greidi, for her yeoman's work at keeping us all organized.

The real credit for this book, of course, goes to all the people whose experiences and collective wisdom make up this guide. There are too many of you to thank individually, of course, but you know who you are. Thanks for sharing.

CREDITS

Page 6:   United Nations' Population Fund Report, 2003.

Page 10: Mark Lino, "Expenditures on Children by Families," Center for Nutrition Policy and Promotion, June 2000.

Page 28: "Taming The "Night Owls," by Kathiann M. Kowalski, *Odyssey*, January 2002, Vol. 11 Issue 1, p19.

Page 30: Erika Karres, ED.D., author of *Mean Chicks, Cliques, and Dirty Tricks*.

Page 32: Susie Walton, Redirecting Children's Behavior Course Instructor.

Page 36: Susie Walton, Redirecting Children's Behavior Course Instructor.

Page 41: Susie Walton, Redirecting Children's Behavior Course Instructor.

Page 42: "Sit the Kids Down . . . And Have Dinner," by Thomas Sexton, *Psychology Today*, Sep/Oct2003, Vol. 36 Issue 5, p 24.

Page 53: Adapted from *Turn it Off and Tune in to Life! Celebrate National TV-Turnoff Week!*

Page 61: "U.S. Children and Teens Spend More Time On Academics," by Diane Swanbrow, University of Michigan, December 6, 2004.

Page 63: College Board Statistics, based on the 2004 tests.

Page 69: Elaine Fantle Shimberg, author of *Blending Families*.

Page 69: Erika Karres, ED.D., author of *Mean Chicks, Cliques, and Dirty Tricks*.

Page 72: Al Parisi, co-author of *Lunch Bag Notes: Everyday Advice From A Dad To His Daughter.*

Page 74: Al Parisi, co-author of *Lunch Bag Notes: Everyday Advice From A Dad To His Daughter.*

Page 76: "Diversity in Word and Deed: Most Teens Claim Multicultural Friends," Teenage Research Unlimited, November 10, 2004.

Page 82: Elaine Fantle Shimberg, author of *Blending Families*.

Page 83: Erika Karres, ED.D., author of *Mean Chicks, Cliques, and Dirty Tricks*.

Page 85: *The 1996 Kaiser Family Foundation Survey on Teens and Sex: What Teens Today Say They Need to Know, and Who They Listen To.*

Page 85: Susie Walton, Redirecting Children's Behavior Course Instructor.

Page 89: Al Parisi, coauthor of Lunch Bag Notes: Everyday Advice From A Dad To His Daughter.

Page 100: *The 1996 Kaiser Family Foundation Survey on Teens and Sex: What Teens Today Say They Need to Know, and Who They Listen To.*

Page 111: Al Parisi, co-author of *Lunch Bag Notes: Everyday Advice From A Dad To His Daughter.*

Page 111: Susie Walton, Redirecting Children's Behavior Course Instructor.

Page 117: Susie Walton, Redirecting Children's Behavior Course Instructor.

Page 129: National Safety Council.

Page 138: Junior Achievement poll.

Page 139: "Kids May Want Control, But Parents Should Be the Driving Force for Car Buying," by R.J. Ignelzi, San Diego Union-Tribune, July 26, 2004.

Page 153: Teenage Research Unlimited, December 1, 2004.

Page 157: "Teenage Girls Rank Shopping Over Dating," by Monifa Thomas, Chicago Sun-Times, September 9, 2004.

Page 160: "Malls Nationwide Setting Curfews for Teens," by Anita Chang, Associated Press, September 17, 2004.

Page 163 : Al Parisi, co-author of *Lunch Bag Notes: Everyday Advice From A Dad To His Daughter.*

Page 168: *A Statistical Portrait of Adolescent Sex, Contraception, and Childbearing, Washington, DC: The National Campaign to Prevent Teen Pregnancy,* Moore, K.A., Driscoll, A.K., & Lindberg, L.D. (1998).

Page 172 : Al Parisi, co-author of *Lunch Bag Notes: Everyday Advice From A Dad To His Daughter.*

Page 178: *Trends in Sexual Activity and Contraceptive Use Among Teens, Washington: National Campaign to Prevent Teen Pregnancy,* Terry, E., & Manlove, J. (2000).

Page 184: *Christian Science Monitor,* December 13, 2004.

Page 188: *Christian Science Monitor,* December 13, 2004.

Page 193: "U.S. Children and Teens Spend More Time on Academics," by Diane Swanbrow, University of Michigan Research- December 6, 2004.

Page 196: W. Bruce Cameron, nationally syndicated columnist and author of *8 Simple Rules For Dating My Teenage Daughter,* and *How to Remodel A Man.*

Page 196: National Institute on Media and the Family, 2004 report.

Page 197: "Fan Club Confessions: Teens Underestimate Influence of Celebrity Idols," by Courtney Bennett, *Psychology Today,* Jan/Feb2002, Vol. 35 Issue 1, p18.

Page 198 : Al Parisi, co-author of *Lunch Bag Notes: Everyday Advice From A Dad To His Daughter.*

Page 200: Adapted from "High School and Youth Trends," The National Institute on Drug Abuse (NIDA).

Page 206: Adapted from "High School and Youth Trends," The National Institute on Drug Abuse (NIDA).

Page 208: National Institute on Drug Abuse (NIDA), 2004.

Page 210: "Studies Find Teenagers Are on Better Behavior, Forgoing Many Vices," by Michelle Quinn, Knight Ridder Newspapers.

Page 221: Elaine Fantle Shimberg, author of *Blending Families.*

HELP YOUR FRIENDS SURVIVE!

Order extra copies of *How to Survive Your Teenager,* or one of our other books*:*

Check your local bookstore, www.hundredsofheads.com, or order here.

Please send me:

_____ copies of *How to Survive Your Teenager* (@$13.95)

_____ copies of *How to Survive A Move* (@$13.95)

_____ copies of *How to Survive Your Marriage* (@$13.95)

_____ copies of *How to Survive Your Baby's First Year* (@$12.95)

_____ copies of *How to Survive Dating* (@$12.95)

_____ copies of *How to Survive Your Freshman Year* (@$12.95)

Please add $3.00 for shipping and handling for one book, and $1.00 for each additional book. Georgia residents add 4% sales tax. Kansas residents add 5.3% sales tax. Payment must accompany orders. Please allow 3 weeks for delivery.

My check for $_____ is enclosed.

Please charge my __ Visa __ MasterCard __ American Express

Name _____

Organization _____

Address _____

City/State/Zip _____

Phone _____E-mail _____

Credit card # _____

Exp. Date _____Signature _____

Please make checks payable to HUNDREDS OF HEADS BOOKS, INC.

Please fax to 212-937-2220, or mail to:

HUNDREDS OF HEADS BOOKS, INC.
#230
2221 Peachtree Road, Suite D
Atlanta, Georgia 30309

www.hundredsofheads.com

HELP WRITE THE NEXT Hundreds of Heads™ SURVIVAL GUIDE!

*Tell us your story about a life experience, and what lesson you learned from it. If we use your story in one of our books, we'll send you a free copy. Use this card or visit **www.hundredsofheads.com**.*

Here's my story/advice on surviving

❏ **A NEW JOB** (years working:_____ profession/job:_____)

❏ **A MOVE** (# of times you've moved: _____)

❏ **A DIET** (# of lbs. lost in best diet: _____)

❏ **A TEENAGER** (ages/sexes of your children: _____)

❏ **DIVORCE** (times married: _____ times divorced: _____)

❏ _____ **OTHER TOPIC** (you pick)

Name _____City/State: _____

❏ Use my name ❏ Use my initials only ❏ Anonymous
(Note: Your entry in the book may also include city/state and the descriptive information above.)

How should we contact you *(this will not be published or shared)*:

e-mail: _____ other: _____

Please mail to:

HUNDREDS OF HEADS BOOKS, INC.
#230
2221 Peachtree Road, Suite D
Atlanta, Georgia 30309

Your story/advice:

ABOUT THE EDITORS

BETH REINGOLD GLUCK is the mother of three teenage boys, all of whom are still in school, still without a police record, and still showing up at home most nights for a good evening meal. She received a master's degree in social work from Washington University in St. Louis, but claims to have received her most valuable motherhood training when working as a unit head at a summer camp. There, she learned to sleep fully clothed in anticipation of late night shenanigans, and to listen for the truth between the lines of explanations and excuses. Beth is a proud Pittsburgher and has lived in Atlanta with her husband, two dogs, and children for the past two decades.

JOEL ROSENFELD is the father of three teenage children, who are responsible for many of the gray hairs on his head. Though both he and his wife, Gail, hold graduate degrees, their children have taught them more about the art of negotiation, anger management, and the impact of hormones on behavior than any of their professors ever did. Earlier in his career, Joel spent six years teaching high school, where he found that he learned as much (if not more) from his students as he taught them. Joel holds a BA from the University of Chicago and an MA from Teachers College, Columbia University.

Other Books from HUNDREDS OF HEADS™ BOOKS

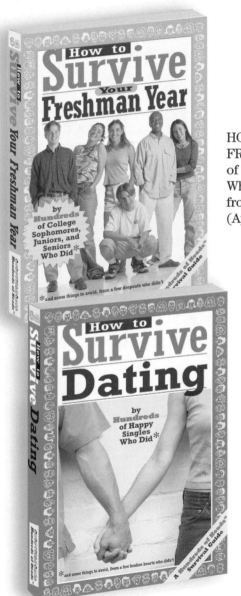

HOW TO SURVIVE YOUR FRESHMAN YEAR . . .by Hundreds of Sophomores, Juniors, and Seniors Who Did (and some things to avoid, from a few dropouts who didn't)™ (April 2004; ISBN 0-9746292-0-0)

HOW TO SURVIVE DATING. . . by Hundreds of Happy Singles Who Did (and some things to avoid, from a few broken hearts who didn't)™ (October 2004; ISBN 0-9746292-1-9)

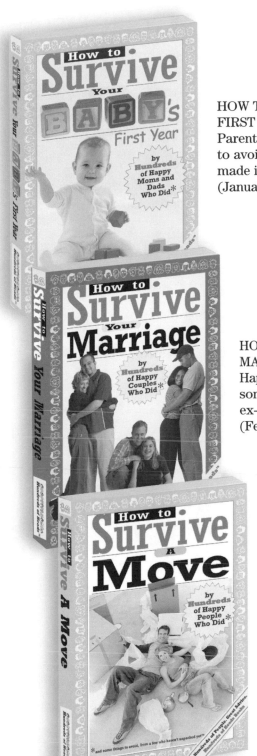

HOW TO SURVIVE YOUR BABY'S
FIRST YEAR . . . by Hundreds of
Parents Who Did (and some things
to avoid, from a few who barely
made it)™
(January 2005; ISBN 0-9746292-2-7)

HOW TO SURVIVE YOUR
MARRIAGE . . . by Hundreds of
Happy Couples Who Did (and
some things to avoid, from a few
ex-spouses who didn't)™
(February 2005; 0-9746292-4-3)

HOW TO SURVIVE A MOVE . . .
by Hundreds of Happy People
Who Did (and some things to
avoid, from a few who haven't
unpacked yet)™
(Spring 2005; 0-9746292-5-1)

VISIT WWW.HUNDREDSOFHEADS.COM

Do you have something interesting to say about marriage, your in-laws, dieting, holding a job, or one of life's other challenges?

 Help humanity—share your story!

 Get published in our next book!

 Find out about the upcoming titles in the HUNDREDS OF HEADS™ survival guide series!

 Read up-to-the-minute advice on many of life's challenges!

 Sign up to become an interviewer for one of the next HUNDREDS OF HEADS™ survival guides!

 Find out about HUNDREDS OF HEADS™ events in your area!

Visit www.hundredsofheads.com today!

Let's Put Our Heads Together— Join the HUNDREDS OF HEADS Team.

✓ Learn more about HUNDREDS OF HEADS Books

✓ Be the first to know when new books are released

✓ Get special offers from HUNDREDS OF HEADS Books

✓ Find out what books we're working on, so that you, too, can get your story in print

Tell us how to reach you: E-mail: _____
We will not publish your e-mail address or forward it to any third parties.

Suggestions/feedback? _____
_____
_____
_____
_____

Because Hundreds of Heads are Better than One!™

Here's my story/advice on surviving

❑ **DATING** ❑ **FRESHMAN YEAR** (college and year of graduation: _____)
❑ **MARRIAGE** (years married: _____) ❑ **A NEW JOB** (years working:_____ profession/job: _____)
❑ **YOUR BABY'S FIRST YEAR** (ages/sexes of your children:_____)
❑ **A MOVE** (# of times you've moved:_____) ❑ **DIVORCE** (times married:_____ times divorced:_____)
❑ **DIET** (# of lbs. you've lost in best diet: _____) ❑ _____ **OTHER TOPIC** (you pick)

Name: _____ City/State: _____

❑ Use my name ❑ Use my initials only ❑ Anonymous
(Your entry in the book may also include city/state and the descriptive information above.)

How should we contact you *(this will not be published or shared)*:
e-mail: _____ other: _____

Here's my story/advice: _____
_____
_____
_____
_____
_____
_____
_____

need more room? visit www.hundredsofheads.com

BUSINESS REPLY MAIL
FIRST-CLASS MAIL   PERMIT NO. 220   ATLANTA, GA

POSTAGE WILL BE PAID BY ADDRESSEE

HUNDREDS OF HEADS BOOKS, INC.
#230
2221 Peachtree Road, Suite D
Atlanta, Georgia 30309

NO POSTAGE
NECESSARY
IF MAILED
IN THE
UNITED STATES

BUSINESS REPLY MAIL
FIRST-CLASS MAIL   PERMIT NO. 220   ATLANTA, GA

POSTAGE WILL BE PAID BY ADDRESSEE

HUNDREDS OF HEADS BOOKS, INC.
#230
2221 Peachtree Road, Suite D
Atlanta, Georgia 30309